Praise for Vera Pezer

"When Vera Pezer takes the time to give you encouragement and advice, you listen. Carefully. Listening to Vera has taught me professionalism as a university employee, confidence as a national team athlete, and competence as a provincial coach. I hear Vera's inimitable voice in the insights expressed in *Smart Curling*, and as I read it, I am reminded of the fundamental strategies I have learned from her. As a bonus, I have also discovered new gems of wisdom to stow away for my future work, athletic, and coaching endeavours."

—*Heather Kuttai, former Paralympic medallist,
Jeux du Canada Games manager*

"Vera was a key part of our coaching team as we prepared for the 1988 Olympics in Calgary. Thanks to the new mental training techniques introduced to us by Vera, we successfully faced the challenges of the first-ever women's curling event in the Olympic Games. This Canadian champ really understands what it takes to be your best!"

—*Linda Moore, Canadian and World Curling Champion,
Olympic Gold Medallist, curling coach*

"Vera helped guide our team to gold in the 1988 Olympics in Calgary, a thrill that will last a lifetime. As our team's sport psychologist, she helped us reach new levels of performance both as individuals and as a team. The skills I acquired then helped fuel my work with athletes in my twelve years as national coach with the Canadian Curling Association. In *Smart Curling*, Vera shares her wisdom, and I have no doubt that the book will enhance the performances of all who read it."

—*Lindsay Sparkes, three-time Canadian Curling Champion, World Champion, Olympic Gold Medallist, and Women's National Team Coach*

"Conversations with Vera Pezer have always had a calming effect on me and other competitive golfers at our club and around the province. Her methods and understanding of the nature of sport have helped me put the game into perspective and boost my confidence. She has certainly enabled me to go out and play with enthusiasm and a set of manageable expectations."

—*Earl Scott, Head Golf Professional, Riverside Country Club, Saskatoon*

SMART CURLING

HOW TO PERFECT YOUR GAME THROUGH
MENTAL TRAINING

VERA PEZER, Ph.D.

FIFTH
HOUSE

Cover and interior design by Brian Smith / Articulate Eye
Cover photo: ©iStockphoto.com/Rueben Schulz
Edited by Geri Rowlatt
Copyedited by Charlene Dobmeier
Proofread by Kirsten Craven

The type in this book is set in Adobe Jenson Pro.

The publisher gratefully acknowledges the support of The Canada Council for the Arts and the Department of Canadian Heritage.

THE CANADA COUNCIL | LE CONSEIL DES ARTS
FOR THE ARTS | DU CANADA
SINCE 1957 | DEPUIS 1957

We acknowledge the financial support of the Government of Canada through the Book Publishing Industry Development Program (BPIDP) for our publishing activities.

Printed in Canada

2008 / 1

First published in the United States in 2008 by
Fitzhenry & Whiteside
311 Washington Street
Brighton, Massachusetts, 02135

Library and Archives Canada Cataloguing in Publication

Pezer, Vera
    Smart curling : how to perfect your game through mental training / Vera Pezer.

Includes bibliographical references and index.

ISBN 978-1-897252-03-1

    1. Curling--Psychological aspects. I. Title.
GV845.P49 2007   796.96401'9   C2007-905823-X

Fifth House Ltd.
A Fitzhenry & Whiteside Company
1511, 1800-4 St. SW
Calgary, Alberta T2S 2S5

1-800-387-9776
www.fitzhenry.ca

Contents

List of Charts and Exercises

Acknowledgements

Smart Curling is the result of contributions from a number of smart people. Publisher Charlene Dobmeier is one of them. Shortly after completing my first book, *The Stone Age: A Social History of Curling on the Prairies*, Charlene suggested that I put together a manuscript on curling psychology. I could take my competitive background, she reasoned, and combine it with my long-time experience as a sport psychologist to write something that would help curlers improve their games. Discussions on book form and content ensued and eventually the project was on. I am grateful to Charlene for her support throughout this and other projects and for her friendship.

Editor Geri Rowlatt deserves thanks. She massaged my initial efforts into a smoother, less pedantic version of *Smart Curling* while maintaining the book's educational integrity. Through our back-and-forth communications, Geri made suggestions that helped to strengthen the book.

I enjoyed working with Fifth House Managing Editor Meaghan Craven. It takes considerable diplomacy to negotiate changes to a manuscript without arousing defensiveness in the person who prepared it. The cheerful, friendly manner Meaghan brought to our discussions resulted in productive exchanges that never became awkward. Meaghan is a diplomat.

My sister, Naomi Selent, did the typing and assisted with additions to the manuscript and editorial changes.

Despite her own career demands, she always completed my material on time, assisting collaboratively, competently, and with good humour even when I obsessed over wording.

I am grateful to Allison Earl, Bob Miller, and Todd Trann for reading the original draft and offering valuable suggestions that improved *Smart Curling*. Each had a different perspective to contribute. Allison is an intelligent, experienced competitor who has curled nationally in women's and mixed competition. A Canadian Curling Association coach of the year, coach of the Stefanie Lawton team, and former Brier competitor, Bob is one of the most astute students of the game I know. Todd, on the other hand, is a relative newcomer to curling. I enjoy assisting him with his game because he shows an enthusiasm and desire to improve that suggests he has a promising curling future.

Finally, I must thank the curlers—beginners, promising juniors, those who aspired to great things, and Canadian, World, and Olympic champions with whom I have worked for more than two decades. I learned as much from them as they ever did from me.

The Right Energy

Mental training is important in all sports, but it is crucial in the game of curling, which is often described as chess on ice. When teams of equal technical ability compete, assuming breaks and bad luck are not factors in the outcome, the team with greater mental toughness and better psychological tools will win. Having this personal control is an enormous confidence builder because the greater mastery you have over yourself, the greater the control you have over a competitive situation. In fact, mental toughness—"the ability to consistently perform toward the upper range of your talent and skill regardless of the competitive circumstances"[1]—improves a team's chances of success, despite adversity.

Whether you're a serious competitor or a curler looking to improve your game, this book will help you become a more complete curler by developing your mental skills using techniques such as concentration, imagery, effecting thinking, and stress management. Sharpening your mental skills will complement your technical and tactical development and improve your on-ice performance. The key to success is accepting what you can't change and developing mastery over what you can, like shot making and psychological self-control. To quote an anonymous source: "We can't change the wind, but we can adjust the sails."

Developing a new and effective mental approach to your game takes dedication and practice, and you're likely to encounter challenges along the way—some personal, some involving teammates, some game related. There are numerous exercises, tips, and suggestions in this book that will help you overcome these common problems. For example, you will learn methods to help you banish negative thoughts, maintain your confidence, manage conflict situations, and use your practice time more effectively. Sometimes, though, no matter how determined you are to change your mindset and how much you practise the recommended techniques, it's not quite enough. If you find yourself in this position, it is important that you consult a sport psychologist for more advice and counseling.

In this chapter, you'll learn about the concept of activation—often labeled excitement—and how motivation and stress can either contribute to or interfere with your on-ice performance. Once you know how to manage and maintain your motivation and stress at an optimum level, you'll be able to build on the physical, tactical, and psychological techniques that you need to become a smart curler.

Curlers, like all athletes, describe the energy involved in competition in a variety of ways. Phrases such as "I'm pumped," "We're ready," or "Let's kick butt" convey a readiness to get a game (or end) underway. But even though these comments are positive, self-affirming, and intended to be motivating, they say little about the *amount* of energy that needs to be directed to performance. The most successful curlers can recognize the level of readiness—of feeling "pumped"—that they need to achieve to perform well. They do this by learning to use positive statements and other strategies to adjust their level of energy throughout the game and by being able to distinguish between and manage different kinds of energy, namely excitement, motivation, and stress.

EXCITEMENT

The concept of excitement (sometimes called activation or arousal) has been associated with performance for nearly a hundred years.[2] This state of general physical and mental energy can range from a feeling of very low excitement to a level that is so high it feels unpleasant and you have a hard time concentrating. It affects performance in the form of an inverted U curve. When your activation is very low, you won't perform well. (Think of playing your regular Monday night club game after a big bonspiel or playdown weekend.) As your excitement increases, your performance will improve to eventually reach a level where you perform your best. But if your excitement gets higher than this optimum level, your performance will deteriorate and you'll miss shots. Missing crucial shots at crucial times because excitement is too high is often referred to as choking.

Even the most serious competitive curlers can lose their focus and concentration when under intense pressure. For example, on the sixth end of the gold medal game of the 2006 Olympics, Finnish skip Markku Uusipaavalniemi faced six Canadian rocks as he threw his final stone. Constant pressure from the Canadian team for five ends combined with this huge amount of granite finally caught up with him. He missed badly. Canada counted six points for a large lead that led to a gold medal. The dramatic miss by Uusipaavalniemi and the sudden, huge opportunity it provided may have pushed the excitement of Canadian skip Brad Gushue beyond his optimum level. With his final stone, he missed a draw that would have given Canada seven points.

Activation or excitement is different for different tasks. Tasks that call for a lower level of strength and more precision and steadiness (like delivering a rock) typically need lower activation for best performance than a task like brushing a rock, which uses larger muscles and calls for greater intensity. The amount of activation is also different for different individuals. Colleen Jones's former championship foursome and Randy Ferbey's record setters have tended to play their best under high levels of activation. Players like these acquire a reputation for performing well in "big" games, and any flat performances they have usually happen earlier in a competition. At the other end of the scale are teams (and individuals) who excel at lower levels of activation and tend to come up short when stakes are highest (later chapters on concentration and stress management offer strategies to change this). Most teams, however, fluctuate between these two extremes, their on-ice success influenced by external events such as ice conditions, mismatched rocks, and the opposing team's performance, and by internal, personal factors such as worrying about performance; and feeling frustrated when things go wrong.

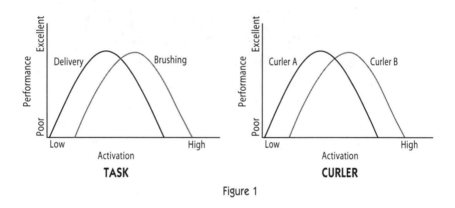

Figure 1

Excitement fluctuates more than skill over a short period of time. It is well known that "A" qualifiers don't win more bonspiels than "B" or "C" qualifiers (who have lost games en route to the playoff). This is probably because "A" teams qualify earlier and lose momentum (activation) over the thirty-six or so hours from when they qualified to when they play their first quarter-final game, while "B" and "C" qualifiers face less down time and are more able to maintain their momentum. Common sense tells us that levels of excitement will fluctuate more over thirty-six hours than a curler's ability to make shots, which is the more stable attribute.

To deal with situations like these, successful curlers acquire tools like imagery and proper breathing to manage their activation level and maximize their performance, much like they learn techniques to develop a consistent in-turn. During a game, your excitement will fluctuate quickly, and sometimes dramatically, in response to on-ice events. Psychological techniques help you control these fluctuations and keep activation as close as possible to your optimum level. One curler I know stands behind the hack for a few seconds just before attempting her shot. She says "relax" while she takes a deep breath and exhales. Because she has learned her optimum activation and recognizes how it feels, she can use breathing and appropriate words to get herself to the appropriate level. This is an important part of her pre-shot routine.

How to Manage Excitement and Maximize Performance

The first step is to learn to recognize your optimum level. This is done by keeping a log to help you determine your pre-game excitement level, which you then compare with your on-ice performance. Keeping a log early in the season is good preparation for the rest of the year. The log included here tracks three elements that contribute to overall activation:

- pre-game physical experiences: you are physically ready and warmed up (strong, flexible) or physically unprepared (butterflies, stiff, tired).

- pre-game thoughts (cognitions): you are focused and ready to play (I am looking forward to this game; I feel good every time I enter this rink) or verbally distracted and unfocused (It's been a hassle to get here on time; I forgot to make a phone call).

- pre-game emotions: you are emotionally connected (happy to connect with your teammates; positive about the game; excited to be going on the ice) or emotionally unconnected (worried about playing well).

Fill in the log for about twenty-five practices and games or until a pre-game excitement assessment becomes part of your routine. The first game (or practice) that you record in your log is your benchmark for your subsequent practices and games. In general, your scores should be lower for practices (even if you are simulating a championship final) than for club games and should increase with the importance of a game. Give your pre-game physical experiences, thoughts, and emotions a rating between 1 and 7, where 1 is very low, 4 is average, and 7 is very high.

Using the log also helps you see if patterns exist in your overall activation. For example, do your pre-game emotions consistently rate higher than your physical symptoms and thoughts? If so, you can target strategies like thought replacement to better control your emotions. If your highest ratings are physical, then strategies like deep breathing and muscle relaxation will help you gain control over this component. The key is to use this log regularly until you feel you can assess yourself without it.

EXCITEMENT LOG

	Date	Game (G) Practice (P)	Opponent (if relevant)	Physical	Thoughts	Emotional	Average	Performance Percentage*
				Activation Level 1-Low 4-Average 7-High				
1								
2								
3								
4								
5								
6								
7								
8								
9								
10								
11								
12								
13								
14								
15								
16								
17								
18								
19								
20								
21								
22								
23								
24								
25								
26								
27								
28								
29								
30								

* When some percentages are not available, rate your performance from 1 to 7, where 1–2 is poor; 3–5 is average; 6–7 is good.

More on Managing Excitement

It's important to recognize that your activation level will fluctuate during a game as circumstances change. Acquiring a big lead can result in lower activation and a tendency to "let up" in a game. Having a big end scored against you can raise or lower your activation significantly. And what about preparing to throw the last rock in an important game? Once you know your pre-game optimum level, you can apply strategies to manage fluctuations throughout a game.

Optimum levels will vary for each curler for different tasks. For example, one player might be a very effective brusher under very high excitement while a teammate is more prone to brushing errors at that level and needs somewhat lower activation. Each curler must learn his or her appropriate optimum levels for tasks like throwing and brushing rocks.

Realistically, it's impossible to control everything in a curling game. Flashed shots, flukes, and "picks" can leave a curler feeling helpless, and your team's shot choice and execution only partially affect your opponent's shots. But you can improve your chances of success by practising mental skills and using them in competition, just as you would technical competencies like delivering a rock, timing shots, or brushing a stone. Skills such as visualization, mental rehearsal, and self-talk are influenced by the level of excitement experienced at the moment, and excitement, in turn, can be modified by the same mental skills. Everything works together. The key is to, first, develop an awareness of what excites you (by using an excitement log), what changes it, and how it feels when it changes and, then, apply the techniques you need to manage it to achieve your best possible performance.

MOTIVATION

Motivation is energy that is directed to a specific goal, rather than a general feeling of excitement. Curlers are motivated to compete for a variety of reasons (goals), which can be extrinsic, like prize money or sponsorships, or intrinsic, like achieving personal standards of excellence. In Canada, jewellery won by Scotties competitors is worn with pride, while Brier competitors value the purple-heart crest that signifies they have represented their province at the Brier. But prize money and crests in themselves are not sufficient goals to produce champions—it is the rewards that accompany a curler's internal motive to succeed that produce champions. True success comes more from an **internal** passion for the game. Without a personal motive to succeed, all the prize money in the world won't ensure a curler's success.

Psychologists have recognized that various internal motives (or drives) are important to performing well, whether on the job, in the classroom, or on a sheet of curling ice. In my academic research and subsequent work with athletes in a variety of sports, I've relied on the motivational theories of Harvard psychologists J. W. Atkinson and his colleagues. They defined three categories of internal motives that relate to performance: the need for achievement; the need for affiliation; and the need for power.[3]

Internal Motives

The need for achievement is crucial to performance. Curlers with a high achievement need to set measurable goals and connect their goals directly to their pursuit of excellence and subsequent success. Brier Champion and Olympic Silver Medalist Kevin Martin is often cited for his commitment to daily practice during the curling season. Kevin and others with this high need value practice and tend to set measurable standards or goals that will motivate them. If eight successive draws to the four-foot ring is Kevin's practice goal, making six of the eight will frustrate him but making eight might motivate him to try for ten, just to see if he can do it. High-need achievers are moderate risk takers—tasks that are too easy have no appeal for them. Kevin would not be challenged by a goal of two draws to the four foot when he knows he can make more. Unrealistically difficult tasks are also of little interest to curlers like Kevin. Pursuing a goal of two hundred consecutive four-foot draws in one practice session would likely be of little interest to him because only twenty shots are required in a game. (If someone offered him a thousand dollars to try, though, it might make a difference.) Monetary incentives aside, high-need achievers are attracted to goals that are difficult but potentially attainable.

Affiliation involves connecting with others, and people with a high need for affiliation value satisfying relationships. They make excellent teammates because they offer acceptance, support, respect, understanding, and friendship and thrive when teammates, coaches, and important others reciprocate. Jan Betker, a member of the World and

Olympic Champion Sandra Schmirler foursome, told me that mutual respect, acceptance, and genuine friendship were key ingredients of their success. Even though other teams possessed similar skill and experience and worked just as hard to be successful, what set the Schmirler team apart was the loyalty and friendship that created an unshakeable bond within the team. Their affinitive chemistry made the team powerful—and successful.

Those who have a high need for power seek dominance. For them, it is all about mastering the sport, dominating opponents, and winning. Whereas curlers with a high need for achievement are likely to express dissatisfaction with a sub par performance and accept the win with less than overall satisfaction, those with high-power needs find small comfort in a well-played game that results in a loss. These curlers are often quite intense in competition and work best with teammates who are not threatened by their emotion. Properly channeled, the need for power contributes energy to a team. Two-time World Champion Rick Folk said that "playing angry" sometimes gave his team an edge. If the crowd was supporting his team's opponent, Rick and his teammates Ron Mills and brothers Tom and Jim Wilson used the situation to their advantage by focusing on sending the crowd home disappointed.

To learn what motivates you, list five reasons why you curl on the log provided here. Then rank each item on your list from 1 to 5 (1 being most important and 5 least important).

MOTIVATION LOG

Date: _____

Rank (1 to 5)	Why I Curl

If your most important reasons for curling involve skill development and acquiring a reputation as a competent competitor, you tend to have a need for achievement. If they focus on your relationships with your teammates, affiliation is more important to you. If your top reasons are to defeat a certain rival or win a provincial championship, you are definitely disposed toward the need for power. It is more likely, though, that your makeup involves all three elements, with one more dominant than the others. Combinations of these three motives among teammates produce the motivational chemistry that makes each team unique. Affiliation within the Schmirler team was undoubtedly high, but to be successful Marcia Gudereit, Joan McCusker, Jan Betker, and Sandra Schmirler also had to bring healthy doses of the need for achievement and for power to the team. Of the three motives, the need for achievement is the most important to performance. Being friendly or setting out to demolish your opponent won't produce success without a commitment to personal achievement.

Understanding your motives for competing helps you in two ways. First, for example, if you recognize that the need for power is your strongest motive, you may decide to give more attention to your relationships with your teammates (affiliation) and set some practice and game performance goals that offer personal satisfaction (achievement). Your satisfaction with the game will increase when defeating your opponent (power) is not your only motive for competing. Second, accepting that teammates bring different motivational strengths to competition will make you more tolerant of motives that differ from yours. Problems commonly result when a curler with a high need to dominate assumes that a teammate with a high need for affiliation does not care as much about being successful. Both qualities are important to a team's success.

The Negative Side of Motives

Clearly, each of these motives has a positive effect on performance, but each also has a negative side. High-need achievers are sometimes motivated as much by fear of failure as by its counterpart, the more positive anticipation of success. Tom Wilson, Rick Folk's second, confessed that the thrill of winning did not motivate him nearly as much as the fear, or hatred, of losing. This can be effective energy—but only if it's not too extreme or doesn't become the sole motivator. Athletes who begin to associate the fear of failure with a positive outcome (winning the region) may develop a tendency to increase that emotion in the hope it will result in an even more successful outcome (winning the province). However, excessive use of such an unpleasant motive eventually leads to a negative effect on performance. I worked with a track athlete whose fear-of-failure motivation had become so overwhelmingly dominant that an event she loved and had excelled at had evolved into a negative experience. Her constant self-criticism over potential failure, which began as motivation, had hampered her performance and eliminated the joy of competition. A need for achievement based on the pursuit of success and the fear of failure is a powerful motivator as long as concerns over failing don't override the more positive side of achievement.

The need for affiliation motivates an athlete to offer and seek friendship and support from teammates, family, and friends. Its negative counterpart is the need to perform well in order to not disappoint others. Athletes who are motivated by the negative side of this need worry that a poor performance will result in a loss of caring and respect from the special people in their life. In extreme cases, this motive, whether imagined or real, can interfere with performance if, for example, an athlete's focus shifts from concentrating on shot execution to wondering what others are thinking. Similarly, the need to dominate others (power) includes the parallel fear of being dominated. If an athlete who needs to dominate assumes that the same motive exists with the same intensity in an opponent, instead of focusing on personal performance, the athlete may be distracted by dwelling on who has greater power.

A certain amount of negative emotion is a normal part of the overall motive to succeed whenever performance of any kind—job, schoolwork, music recital, or curling—is evaluated. For athletes, fear of failure, fear of losing the respect of others, and fear of being dominated exist to varying degrees, especially when the stakes are high. Yet, although fear is not pleasant, it does not hamper performance unless, as with the track athlete, it becomes excessive. The key to dealing with fear is to accept some fear as a normal part of the decision to enter a competitive environment.

Understanding Your Performance Motives

The Atkinson model of performance motivation is an excellent fit with curling. A high need for achievement motivates serious curlers to accomplish their set goals. Curling is a social game that encourages affiliation with others, and relationships are important, especially between teammates. Competition is about power, demonstrated through mastery of the game and defeating opponents who are out to defeat you. The better you understand your performance motives, the greater personal control you bring to competition.

For a better understanding of your performance motives, try the "Will to Win" questionnaire. Although athletes in any team sport can use it, I designed it especially for curlers. The fourteen items on the questionnaire reflect a curler's motives for competing. For each item, check True or False, and then use the scoring key at the end of the questionnaire to determine how many of your answers contribute to your will to win.

The higher you score, the higher your Will to Win (ww). If you had one to three correct answers, you have a low ww; a score of four to seven means you have a moderate ww; and eight to fourteen correct answers reflect your high ww. Based on my research, the most successful curlers score the highest on the Will to Win questionnaire and on curling skill tests. Curlers with moderate skill and a high ww are more successful than those with a high skill level and a lower ww. In other words, the Will to Win is a powerful motivator that offsets moderate skill limitations—but a high Will to Win cannot produce success without a fairly high degree of skill. Both work together. Aspiring champions who have a high ww practise diligently, and seek strong competition have the best chance of success.

The fourteen items on the questionnaire all relate to Atkinson's motives: items 2, 4, 8, 11, and 14 relate to the need for achievement; items 6, 7, 10, and 13 to the need for affiliation; and items 1, 3, 5, 9, and 12 to the need for power. As you did with the Motivation Log (p. 13), you can examine your answers to these fourteen items to see if you lean toward a particular motive or if your reasons for competing are balanced with all three motives (see The Role of Personality in Chapter 3).

THE WILL TO WIN

Instructions: Check True or False for each item as it applies to you. Answer as honestly as you can and don't spend too much time on any item. Your first reaction is generally the most accurate.

True	False		
[ ]	[ ]	1.	I hate to lose.
[ ]	[ ]	2.	I get very upset at myself when I play poorly.
[ ]	[ ]	3.	I am more likely to swear when we're losing than when we're winning.
[ ]	[ ]	4.	I don't mind trying different game strategies even if they cause us to lose.
[ ]	[ ]	5.	I go into most games thinking we're going to win.
[ ]	[ ]	6.	I sometimes feel sorry for opponents during a game.
[ ]	[ ]	7.	I don't mind when my teammates play poorly.
[ ]	[ ]	8.	A team can be considered successful without winning.
[ ]	[ ]	9.	Winning is the main reason for competing.
[ ]	[ ]	10.	I am more concerned with having fun than with winning.
[ ]	[ ]	11.	Losing a well-played game is satisfying.
[ ]	[ ]	12.	The main reason for practising is to win.
[ ]	[ ]	13.	I don't mind when my teammates give less than 100 per cent.
[ ]	[ ]	14.	It really hurts to lose a game we should have won.

Scoring Key:

Question	Value	Score
1	T=1; F=0	_____
2	T=1; F=0	_____
3	T=1; F=0	_____
4	T=0; F=1	_____
5	T=1; F=0	_____
6	T=0; F=1	_____
7	T=0; F=1	_____
8	T=0; F=1	_____
9	T=1; F=0	_____
10	T=0; F=1	_____
11	T=0; F=1	_____
12	T=1; F=0	_____
13	T=0; F=1	_____
14	T=1; F=0	_____

Total _____

STRESS

Seventy years ago, stress researcher Hans Selye introduced the concept of General Adaptation Syndrome (GAS), which identified three stages of the stress response: the alarm reaction, the resistance stage, and the exhaustion stage. The alarm reaction (sometimes called "flight or fight") consists of a rush of adrenaline and readiness for action. For instance, think about how you feel just before going onto the ice for an important game. During the resistance stage, the body mobilizes its resources to cope with the stressor. Curlers often describe how they settle down once they are on the ice and the game begins. If the body's resources are not sufficiently maintained during this stage, the next stage, which Selye called exhaustion, is reached. Curlers can become exhausted if they don't eat well, relax enough, and prepare themselves mentally between games and during a long round-robin or playoff stretch. Once this occurs, they have trouble bringing an appropriate level of energy to a game, typically by coming out "flat" or over-compensating in an overly energetic way. Mental lapses like timing errors or strategy mistakes are more likely to occur in the exhaustion stage.

The potential negative outcomes of the syndrome make it essential for you to know what causes you stress when you curl, especially competitively. Once you know the sources of your stress, you can learn to recognize their symptoms and then use techniques such as relaxation and self-talk to help you maintain your appropriate level of competitive stress. Like the fears of failure, disappointment, and being dominated that were described by

Atkinson, stress—as long as it is controlled—should be accepted as a normal part of the competitive curling environment. In competitive curling, too little stress is as problematic as too much stress. Some stress is positive and energizing (like winning a close game), and in many ways competitive curlers can be considered "stress seekers."

Sources of Stress

Curling has three sources of stress: environmental, physical, and emotional (thoughts/feelings). The severity of stress depends on the importance of the task, the duration of the stress, and the number of stressors a curler is experiencing. All three types of stress (and their severity) can affect your performance negatively unless you use coping strategies to keep them at a manageable level. An example of an environmental stressor is changing ice conditions or an opponent at the hog line who moves every time you begin your delivery. Fatigue or a sore back is a physical stressor, while worry about your in-turn, a problem at work, or a new babysitter is an emotional stressor. The severity of a stressor depends on the situation. Obviously, a provincial final (compared to a Tuesday club game) puts greater stress on a curler who wants to perform well, but an extra end in a crucial game also adds stress and a week-long, round-robin competition provides more prolonged stress.

To help you identify your sources of stress, use the following sheet to list all the stressors that you are likely to encounter during the curling season. Add others to the list as the season evolves. One or two examples are given to get you started.

SOURCES OF STRESS

ENVIRONMENTAL	PHYSICAL	EMOTIONAL
Tricky ice	*Chronic knee injury*	*Worry about playing well*
Mismatched rocks	*Not in physical condition*	*Let teammates down*

Symptoms of Stress

Most of us aren't very good at identifying our stress symptoms. For instance, a curler may worry when she suddenly discovers that it is only ten minutes to game time rather than the twenty minutes or so she usually needs to prepare. By worrying, she may be only vaguely aware of the anxiety and physical tension that her perceived lack of preparation time is creating and be less focused on how best to use her available time.

The experience of stress can involve one or a combination of physiological or behavioural symptoms, as well as thoughts and emotions. Use the following checklist to determine your main stress symptoms as you experience them while curling. A number of symptoms appear on the list (and there's room for you to add more). Use a 7-point scale to rate each symptom you experience, where 1–2 = low stress, 3–5 = moderate stress, and 6–7 = high stress. First, complete the pre-practice column just before a curling practice. Then, in the pre-game column, either recall your most recent important game and rate your stress just before that game or complete the rating before your next important game. Rate only those symptoms that apply to you and add any others that you may experience.

Once you've identified your primary symptoms and their sources, you can maintain your stress at an optimum level by applying the breathing exercises and the relaxation, visualization, thought stopping, and self-talk techniques described later in this chapter.

SYMPTOMS OF STRESS CHECKLIST

Stress: 1–2 Low   3–5 Moderate   6–7 High

SYMPTOM	PRE-PRACTICE STRESS LEVEL	PRE-GAME STRESS LEVEL
Tenseness		
Headache		
Distracted		
Tiredness		
Weakness		
Nausea		
Need to go to the bathroom		
Anxiety		
Helplessness		
Lack of confidence		
Anger		
Impatience		
Fear of playing poorly		
Negative thoughts		
Indigestion		
Uncommunicative		
Very talkative		
Nervousness		
Reluctance to warm up		
Pain—knee, neck, back?		
Low energy		
Obsessive thinking		
Ritual behaviour		
Irritability		
Trouble concentrating		

Environmental Stressors

Environmental stressors such as game delays, distracting comments from others, or mismatched rocks are external stimuli with the potential to affect your thoughts and emotions and how you respond physically. There are three ways to handle environmental stressors: you can change the environment, manage it better, or briefly leave the curling environment.

Changing the Environment

Switching rocks partway through a game to ensure that the skip has the best matched pair is an example of changing the environment. Whether the difference between the rocks is real or imagined, switching rocks can minimize the stress a skip can experience if he or she concentrates too much on what the rocks are doing rather than the shots to be made. If a skip's excessive concern about rocks occurs game after game, a more serious problem—a loss of self-confidence—may exist and needs to be addressed (see the Imagery and Thought stopping sections of this chapter). Rocks differ, and it is sound strategy to pay reasonable attention to matching them and, when necessary, switching them, but over-attention to this indicates anxiety that has gone too far (see the Self-talk and Making the "Irrational" Rational sections of this chapter).

Managing the Environment

Good teams find ways to change the environment when they can. However, when the environment can't be changed, teammates usually work together to find ways to manage it better. Using the ten-minute, pre-game on-ice practice to throw both turns lets team members read the ice and time rocks for a final check on their consistency. Having a well-thought-out plan for the ten-minute practice allows a team to gather good information on how to manage the on-ice environment.

Preparing a plan to contend with time clocks is another example of managing the environment better. Some teams try to play more conservatively in early ends to "bank" time for later in the game. Others start aggressively, with the intention of playing more conservatively when they need to. In both cases, the goal is to ensure there is enough time to devote to ends where numerous rocks are in play and to late ends in a close game.

Recently, some teams have moved away from traditional play where the skip calls the game and throws last rocks and the third holds the broom for skip shots. Teams hoping to improve should look at the Randy Ferbey and Colleen Jones's teams. With the experienced Ferbey calling shots and the superb shot-maker (and better brusher) David Nedohin throwing last rocks, Ferbey's team has enjoyed exceptional bonspiel, Brier, and World Championship success. Jones's championship run that had Kim Kelly throwing third rocks and lead Nancy Delahunt holding the broom for skip shots contributed to their five Canadian Championships in six years. By being innovative, these teams accomplished two things: first, responsibility (and pressure) was distributed more evenly within the team and, second, team skills could be applied where they would be most effective (Delahunt with her shot-calling and Nedohin with his sweeping and shot-making). In recent work with junior teams and their coaches, I have encouraged coaches to remain open-minded about responsibilities within the team. Flexibility and receptiveness to change offer the best chances of managing what is often an unpredictable curling environment.

The 1992 Olympics provided one of the best examples of the importance of managing an unpredictable environment. Kevin Martin and Julie Sutton, Canadian champions from 1991, represented Canada in Albertville, France. Curling, a demonstration sport, had organization, fan interest, and media coverage far short of the standard achieved in 1988 in Calgary and later after the game gained medal status. Ice conditions were deplorable in Pralognan-La-Vanoise, a ski resort in the Alps about 50 kilometres from Albertville. One sheet of ice, under water, could not be played on during the entire competition. Practice times and games were rescheduled as teams coped with major uncertainty, especially early in the competition. Performances suffered and the sport of curling—attempting to achieve medal status—did not showcase itself well.

The two Canadian teams, more accustomed than the Europeans to solid event planning and excellent playing conditions, had to manage circumstances they had never before encountered. Kevin Martin finished fourth and the Sutton team, relying on sheer determination, earned a medal. After finishing first in its pool at 3–0, the team suffered a heart-breaking loss to Norway's Dordi Nordby. With the loss, the gold medal opportunity disappeared. I still remember Canada's third, Jodie Sutton, telling her teammates that she was determined to return home with a medal. That comment, more than anything, inspired the Canadian team to a 9–3 win over Denmark. Julie and Jodie Sutton, assisted by Melissa Soligo and Kari Wilms, earned bronze medals through a gold medal effort in managing a difficult environment.

Leaving the Environment

Just as curlers look for ways to change their environment or manage it to their advantage, they also benefit from breaks from competition, whether planned during the season or imposed by summer and an end to the curling season. A time-out can be as simple as leaving the rink between bonspiel or playdown games. A brief break away from the rink to have lunch, relax, discuss the past game, and plan for the next one will be more private and constructive and have fewer distractions than if it takes place at the rink.

Saskatchewan's Sherry Anderson used this strategy to good advantage prior to her 2004 provincial final against Jan Betker. After playing extremely well in the morning game to reach the final, the team adjourned to the home of their driver. Lunch and a short rest allowed team members to turn their attention to the final game. After briefly reviewing the technical items that needed to be remembered, they focused on their mental approach to the final.

It was important to continue the momentum they had developed during the semi-final against Amber Holland. Because everyone had played well earlier, they decided to treat the semi-final and final not as separate games but as one long game, with the current pause in play viewed more like a fifth-end break. With the idea planted that the afternoon final was a continuation of a solid morning effort, the team continued its steady play and Sherry Anderson, Kim Hodson, Sandra Mulroney, and Donna Gignac went on to represent Saskatchewan at the Canadian Championship in Red Deer. In this case, getting away from the curling environment for a few hours was time well spent.

From the standpoint of the entire season, enthusiasm for the game always seems keener in October after a summer break. Although teammates prepare their seasonal plans during the summer and socialize to stay connected, the fall always brings fresh passion and renewed optimism for the coming season. Some teams play well with few pauses during the season. Others plan an occasional weekend off to avoid burnout and to be fresh for playdowns. Each team is unique, but experience suggests that most curlers benefit from occasional breaks, even for a few days. A time out to attend to the demands of work or school allows curlers to refocus for competition. While watching the Olympic Trials in Halifax in 2005, I wondered whether over-preparation contributed to the less-than-sharp performances by some of the teams whose previous records suggested they should do well. Over-preparation can produce "flatness" in a team that is as stressful as the anxiety of under-preparation. Brief periods away from the game decrease the chances of burnout and contribute to a team's "plan to peak" at the most important time of the season.

As a team, it's important to recognize external stressors so that you and your teammates can change or manage as many of them as possible. It's even more important, though, to know your personal stress threshold. The next section introduces some stress management strategies that you can use to overcome the symptoms you earlier identified in the Symptoms Checklist.[4]

Stress Management Strategies

Athletes usually experience more than one stress symptom. Some are physical, like sleeplessness or muscular tension; others, like irritability or impatience, are emotional. These may be accompanied by stress-contributing thoughts, like frequently recalling a missed shot or the inability to concentrate. Curlers who learn and apply appropriate stress-management techniques to symptoms as they occur can manage their stress more successfully. For example, if you have trouble sleeping, listening to a relaxation recording helps. Learning how to stop a negative thought and replace it with a positive concept is another example of effective stress management.

Physical stress management strategies are particularly important. As well as controlling symptoms that are primarily physical, these strategies induce relaxation, which makes us more receptive to techniques designed to reduce stress that primarily involves our thoughts and emotions. Taking one or two deep breaths as you tell yourself to "relax" makes it easier to replace a thought of a missed shot with that of a successful one. In the same way as you work on the correct release for your in-turn, you need to practise stress reduction techniques for them to be effective. Mastering several techniques that work together gives you the self-control you need to deal with stressful and difficult competitive circumstances.

Physical Strategies

Two basic physical stress management strategies are included here: controlled breathing and muscular relaxation.[5]

CONTROLLED BREATHING

Most of the time, we pay little attention to how we breathe. In fact, poor habits like holding your breath or shallow breathing make it harder to manage stressful situations. Noticing how you breathe and learning techniques to deepen and slow your breathing not only help you relax but also make it easier for you to use other stress reduction techniques like imagery and thought stopping.

BREATHING EXERCISE

- Stand with your feet about shoulder width apart.

- Check your neck and shoulder muscles for tension. Let your head drop toward your chest.

- Relax your jaw—your teeth and lips should be slightly apart.

- Concentrate on your body.

- Inhale—slowly and deeply—through your nose to a count of three.

- Hold your breath for a second or two.

- Now, take three or four seconds to let the air out slowly through your mouth and say "relax" to yourself.

- Inhale through your nose and exhale through your mouth two or three more times—slowly and deeply—and say the word "relax" each time you exhale.

- Relax.

- Now, refocus and prepare to compete.

+ This exercise is useful just before game time. Once you master it, you can take a single deep breath and slowly exhale it just before delivering a rock.

+ For variety, concentrate on the centre of your body and imagine there is a light inside it. As you inhale, the light becomes brighter; as you exhale, the light becomes dimmer.

MUSCULAR RELAXATION

Muscle relaxation exercises vary. Some have you begin by tensing your muscles in a particular spot (such as clenching your fist), and then completely relaxing that muscle group. Different muscles are tensed and relaxed, in turn, from one end of your body to the other. Another technique eliminates the first step (tensing) and has you focus only on relaxing all of your muscle groups. Others combine muscle relaxation with deep breathing and rely on cue words like "relax," which is effective when your stress is concentrated in one part of your body, like the neck, shoulders, or arms. Deep breathing combined with a focus on relaxing specific muscles and using a cue word to trigger relaxation is a powerful technique that, once learned, requires only two to three minutes to be effective.

The following exercise involves relaxing your entire body. It takes about twenty minutes to complete and one to two weeks of daily practice to learn. You can use it to help you sleep or relax between games when time allows. Once you master this exercise, you can modify it by concentrating on relaxing certain muscles combined with deep breathing and cue words. Instead of just reading the instructions, prepare a recording to guide you through the relaxation steps.

RELAXATION EXERCISE[6]

(Note: An ✳ represents a ten-second pause)

- Spend a little time getting as comfortable as you can. Let the chair or area where you are lying support your body. Move around until you find a position where your muscles don't have to work to hold you. While you're finding a good position, loosen any tight clothing. You may want to slip out of your shoes. Allow your eyes to close and relax.

- Allow your mouth to open for a moment and move your jaw slowly and easily from side to side . . . Now let your mouth close, keeping your teeth slightly apart. As you do this, take a deep breath . . . and slowly let the air slip out.

- Take another deep breath . . . As you breathe out, silently say "relax." Let the air slip out easily and automatically. By now you should be feeling calmer. Carry on breathing slowly and deeply. ✳ The more you relax, the slower your breathing becomes. Your eyes are closed, you are breathing slowly and deeply . . . and you are relaxed.

- Focus your attention on your right forearm and hand. Relax these muscles. Feel the forearm and hand become warm and heavy, warm and heavy. Relaxed, warm, and heavy. Let this feeling flow to your upper arm. The warmth, the heaviness, the relaxation. Slow and effortless breathing. Let your body go and relax. Focus on your left hand and forearm. Feel the same warmth and heaviness as your muscles relax. With each breath, tension dissipates. This warm, relaxed feeling flows into the upper arm. Warmth and heaviness spread through it. ✳ Continue until both arms are totally supported by the surface you are resting on. There is no effort on your part. ✳ Let this relaxation flow from both arms across the shoulders and up your neck. With each breath this relaxation flows further up your face. You feel your jaws, ✳ lips, ✳ tongue, ✳ cheeks, ✳ eyes ✳ relax. The relaxation continues to flow upward as you relax your forehead, ✳ eyebrows, ✳ and top of your head. The muscles are relaxed and heavy. Each slow, effortless breath brings relaxation to your head, ✳ face, ✳ neck, ✳ shoulders. ✳ Now this feeling begins to flow down to the chest and upper back. When this happens you become more aware of your slow effortless abdominal breathing, of your slow even heart rate. ✳ Your upper body is supported totally by the surface you're resting on. There is no effort on your part to hold your body in its present position. Let this relaxation flow down through your abdomen ✳ and lower back. ✳ Your lower torso and everything within it are relaxed and heavy. ✳ Let the feeling go down through your hips, ✳ thighs, ✳ calves, and feet. ✳

- Relaxed, warm, and heavy. Feel yourself spread out as you relax. Let the surface you're resting on support your total body. No effort from you is needed to hold it. Your breathing is slow, effortless, and abdominal. Your heart rate is slow and even. ✳ Beginning at the top of your head, focus on each part of your body and feel it relax more as you attend to it. When you reach your toes, enjoy this state for a while.

(One minute of silence)

- When you are ready to return to a state of alertness, count backward from five to one. Five ... four ... three (relaxed and alert) ... two (mentally wide awake) ... one. Then, bend and stretch your arms, move your head from side to side, and open your eyes. When you open your eyes, you will be fully awake, alert, calm, relaxed, and full of energy, and you'll feel good about yourself.

In his work with alpine skiers, psychologist Dr. Richard Suinn coined the term "visual motor behavioral rehearsal" (VMBR) to describe the relaxation technique he developed to manage activation. He combined that technique with other strategies like mental rehearsal to help skiers achieve top performances. Other sport consultants have used VMBR to help Olympic medalists like figure skater Michelle Kwan and downhill skier Tommy Moe improve their execution. What works for skaters and skiers will also work for curlers.

Mental Strategies

The deep breathing and muscular relaxation exercises you've just learned make it easier to use stress-reduction techniques that will help you control the thoughts and feelings that are the real contributors to stress. Environmental events like a burned rock or a teammate's irritating behaviour do not, in themselves, stress you. Stress results from how you feel about your teammate's behaviour and how you manage yourself physically and emotionally to cope with it. Albert Ellis[7] was one of the first psychologists to propose that how we interpret events, not the events themselves, contributes to the emotions we experience. His work gained wide acceptance because he suggested that not only are we capable of changing how we feel physically and cognitively, but once we are aware of our physical sensations, thoughts, and emotions, we can also take action to change them. It is all about personal awareness and control.

Six techniques—imagery, thought stopping, self-talk, making the "irrational" rational, sharing stress, and time management—are described next. They will help you control stress caused primarily by how you think and feel about the curling environment.

IMAGERY

You use imagery whenever you create mental images, daydreams, and memories or communicate silently to yourself using words and pictures. Psychologists use imagery in many ways, including treating illness and anxiety. As you'll see later, specific visualization (like the position of your foot as it slides) and rehearsal (mentally rehearsing an entire sequence like a complete delivery or playing the entire end of a game) can be useful tools to improve performance. For now, imagery is offered as a technique to help you cope with the stress of competition.

To be effective, imagery should be done in four steps.

1. Lie in a quiet place where you won't be interrupted for twenty to thirty minutes. Loosen your clothing and close your eyes.

2. Use deep breathing or muscular relaxation to relax any muscles that seem tense.

3. Create a peaceful picture, developing it as fully as you can by using all your senses: sight, hearing, smell, touch, and taste. Your picture can be of a familiar place that you already associate with relaxation and tranquility or one that you create. Try something like this:

Imagine a path, lined with pine trees, along a lake. You decide to sit down on a bench and watch the sun set over the lake. See the green of the pine trees, the lake with small ripples caused by a bit of a breeze. Watch the sky change to combinations of orange, crimson, and yellow as the sun slowly sets. Notice the few clouds near the horizon. What sounds do you hear? Squirrels chattering to each other? Bird calls? Can you smell newly mowed grass in the evening air? Do you feel the roughness of the pine cone in your hand? Now that you are in perfect harmony with nature, you decide to savour some mints you have in your pocket. Are they spearmint or peppermint?

4. As the scene develops, occasionally talk quietly to yourself, using positive relaxing phrases such as "I feel calm" or "Tension is leaving me."

NOTES

+ Some people begin to feel the effects of imagery quickly; others require a few weeks of regular practice.

+ Use imagery two or three times a day to start. Try doing it first thing in the morning and last thing at night.

+ If you have trouble experiencing all your senses, just focus on those you can create. Eventually, with practice, you should be able to use all five senses in your imagery.

- It's often helpful to play soft music. Pick a favourite piece or try different combinations. The music should be quiet, with a slow tempo. Some athletes make a recording of several arrangements to play while they relax and use imagery.

- Once you're able to use imagery in a relaxed state, you can use it in other places, like driving to the rink or in the dressing room before game time and just after your warm-up.

THOUGHT STOPPING

Negative and anxiety-provoking thoughts, if they occur frequently or the same thought keeps reoccurring, contribute to stress. To stop your unwanted thoughts, follow these four steps:

1. Become aware of stressful thoughts. Decide whether, given the circumstances, a thought is reasonable ("The roads are really icy. I won't drive today.") or a problem that you'd like to stop ("We have trouble winning a final game.").

2. If it's a problem, focus on it briefly.

3. Interrupt the thought by saying "stop" loudly if circumstances allow; if not, imagine yourself saying "stop" in a loud voice.

4. Substitute the negative thought with a positive statement that contradicts the thought you want to remove. For example, substitute "We won the Parktown Classic last year." for "We have trouble winning final games."

+ Prepare a list of several positive statements—they can lose impact if they're used repeatedly. If, after trying it for a while, a statement is not effective, try another one.

+ If the word "stop" is not working in your imagination or you find it embarrassing to say it aloud, find another technique, like snapping your fingers. Or try clenching your fist as you silently say "stop," then unclench it, say the word "relax," and use your positive statement.

+ It takes time to stop a thought, especially one that's been part of your repertoire for some time. The key is to catch it and replace it as consistently as you can.

SELF-TALK

Self-talk is a variation of the thought-stopping technique. It uses positive statements to counteract stress that results from negative thoughts and feelings but doesn't require you to say "stop" to distract yourself from a stressful thought. Instead, you simply identify and list your unproductive thoughts and feelings and write counteracting statements to say to yourself.

Look back at the Sources of Stress sheet that you completed earlier in this chapter. For each stressful thought and feeling you identified, prepare one that counteracts it. Then, when you notice the negative thought, replace it with that one.

Examples

"I'm so nervous that my legs feel weak and rubbery." vs. "I've felt this way before and played well."

"I hate this feeling of tension just before a game." vs. "I don't like feeling tense, but I love the challenge of competition."

- If you're having trouble finding positive statements, do this exercise with your teammates. You can help each other develop lists that are both helpful and meaningful.

MAKING THE "IRRATIONAL" RATIONAL

This is another thought-replacement technique. Most of us constantly engage in self-talk (the internal communication we use to get through daily life) and most of the time our self-talk is accurate. Sometimes, though, we misinterpret it, then make mistakes in judgment and experience distress. Common traps usually involve words like "should" ("I should practise today, but I don't feel like it") or "never" ("We never seem to play well against this team"). Carried to its extreme, we impose perfectionist standards on ourselves that leave us feeling guilty about not practising and anxious about playing certain teams.

Irrational thoughts, like problematic thoughts, usually occur because we blame our frustration and stress on external causes (such as the team that we "never" play well against). But, in fact, it's our interpretation of these external causes (not the causes themselves) that becomes irrational and causes stress. If you tend to "catastrophize" a specific event, a Homework Sheet[8] like the one found on the following page will help you challenge and overcome your irrational thoughts. The sheet is filled out to give you an example of how to use it. To put together your own sheet, choose an upcoming event and then fill in each category (Event, Rational Thought, and so on). Refer to the sheet whenever the irrational thought you've identified begins to take over.

HOMEWORK SHEET

Event: Playing a provincial final in two hours.

Rational Thoughts: "This is a stressful time. I'll do some things to relax and prepare for the game."

Irrational Thoughts: "I'm afraid we'll lose again because we lost the last provincial final."

Effect of Irrational Thoughts: Worry—fear—anxiety

Challenge Irrational Thought:

+ **Identify it:** It will be "awful" to lose again.

+ **Is there rational support for the thought:** "No. We don't lose every game we play."

+ **Evidence that the thought is false:** "We win more games than we lose. We have won bonspiel finals and a previous provincial final."

+ **Evidence that the thought is true:** "Not really. We have lost some finals, but we have also won some."

+ **The most catastrophic thing that could happen:** "We might lose the game."

+ **Outcome of the catastrophe:** "We'll be disappointed, but we'll survive."

+ **Good things to think about:** "We have a chance to win. Lots of other teams would love to be in our place."

+ Patterns of thinking evolve over time and can be difficult to change. If you accept that stress is a normal part of competition but want to change what you believe is problematic thinking, commit yourself to working with the homework sheet on a regular basis.

+ If you're reluctant to accept that your thinking influences the emotions you experience and the homework sheet isn't helping, try talking to your coach or a trusted teammate.

+ If all else fails, consult a sport psychologist.

> "Courage is resistance to fear, mastery of fear, not absence of fear."
> *Mark Twain*

SHARING STRESS

Talking with someone you trust who is a good listener can be an effective way to alleviate stress symptoms. But even though "getting something off your chest" is therapeutic, it's even more helpful if the conversation provides you with some new thinking and options to consider.

Make reaching a decision the goal of your conversation with your confidant. If, for example, you want to talk to a teammate about behaviour you find bothersome, plan with your confidant when and how you will do this and the outcome you want. If you feel stressed because you missed with your in-turn during the last game, your goal would be to decide the best person to ask to help you evaluate your delivery before the next game.

Use moderation in discussing negative feelings with your teammates. Frustration is a normal and an unavoidable part of competition, and your teammates often know when you are showing signs of stress and behave in ways that are helpful. Knowing when and how to say the right thing, whether technical or something humorous to lighten the moment, is a powerful team dynamic. Continuously relying on teammates to help you feel better, though, simply adds to the pressure on them. They are dealing with their own competitive stressors, and your negative feelings can be distracting and contagious and escalate overall team stress. Team communication is discussed in more detail in Chapter 3, but for now it is important for you to understand that although honesty and openness with teammates is vital, your teammates are not responsible for solving your problems. Consulting your coach, a trusted friend, or a family member is a better choice.

Develop a plan for those days when timing or circumstances make it hard to find a confidant. Something as simple as a decision to phone home at the end of the day helps you relax because you have a coping strategy. You have not succumbed to your stressors. You have simply "parked" them and will deal with them at a more appropriate time.

TIME MANAGEMENT

Curlers often have to balance the time they need to commit to practice and competition with the time they need to manage the other demands in their lives. Practice ice is available at 4 PM but your children have to be picked up after school. A bonspiel weekend conflicts with an anniversary or the staff Christmas party. You have a 6:30 PM super league game, and it is 5 o'clock and a project at work, due the next day, is not done. What do you do?

Problems with time management typically result either from competing demands or ineffective time management skills. Constant rushing, lateness, vacillation, and procrastination are common signs of poor time management, which, in turn, leads to impatience, frustration, fatigue, and other stress-related symptoms. The key to managing your busy life is to plan and prioritize.

> **Planning:** Along with your seasonal plan for curling (practices, meetings, bonspiels, playdowns), you need weekly and daily planners that list your curling activities and all your other demands. Your weekly planner should include activities for several days: dentist appointment, parent-teacher meeting, team practice, grocery shopping, and so on. It provides the framework for a daily list that you complete in a few minutes each day. Time management-related stress is often due to chronically feeling behind and not looking for specific reasons associated with the pressure to "catch up." Your daily list takes pressure off you because it helps keep you on track, gives you feedback that things are getting done (even when something unexpected happens), and shows that you are in control of events.

> **Prioritizing:** Look at your planning list and decide which activities you must do and which ones you can delegate to someone or defer to another time. If a friend can pick up your children from school, you can make your 4 PM practice. Maybe the date for an anniversary celebration can

be changed. If it can't, send flowers or a special e-mail or book time together at a later date. Can you take your work project home and finish it after curling or go into work early the next morning to complete it? We juggle demands all the time, but our perception that we are not in control of them causes more distress than the actual demands. Identifying what has to be done, prioritizing those things, and having back-up plans will help keep you on schedule and avoid bringing outside distractions to the rink.

To allow you to focus on curling, a good support network of family, friends, and co-workers is invaluable. In my experience, co-workers happily assumed my administrative and teaching responsibilities so I could focus on winning Canadian championships. Sandra Schmirler and her teammates were always quick to acknowledge the child care provided by their husbands and parents that helped them win the World Championship and the Olympics. Clearly, the pressure of competition is made more manageable by supportive "fans"—both those at the rink and those tending to demands at home.

Successful competitive curlers have generally formed a balance in their life and their sport. Their dedication to the game is matched by a strong commitment to family and career. Children accept parental absences to curl when they know that a ski trip or a trip to Disneyland is their prize at the end of the season. Keeping a healthy balance allows the game to be a priority but not at the expense of other important things. To paraphrase the words of Brier and World Champion Wayne Middaugh: "When I get home, my kids will still love me whether or not I just won."

The next chapter takes a more in-depth look at imagery and self-talk and introduces some techniques to help you concentrate more effectively. These psychological techniques combined with the motivation and physical skills that you bring to your game will help you become the best curler you can be.

Mental Training Techniques that Work

As you know from the first chapter, self-talk and imagery influence your motivation and help manage your activation and stress levels. In this chapter, you'll learn how these techniques, along with concentration, work with your physical and tactical skills to boost your on-ice performance and make you a smarter curler.

When you think about curling practice, you likely envision shot-making, videotaping, sweeping drills, and strategy talks. Recently, though, coaches, athletes, and trainers in many sports have accepted and endorsed mental training as part of practice, and curling is no exception. Obviously, most of your practice still happens on the ice, but you should also be sitting quietly in an armchair at home visualizing curling shots and competitive strategies. Psychological preparation is now considered vital to on-ice skill development. In fact, without deliberately planning to do so, you probably take practice and game experiences home and think about them later. Since you already rehearse your game in an impromptu way, developing a more deliberate approach to mental rehearsal makes sense.

Concentration is the ability to focus on an important task without being influenced by external or internal distractions, and it is essential to performance. Successful people in many areas of life are often recognized for their high level of concentration (what some athletes describe as being "in the zone"). Andrea Schmid and Erik Peper[9] tell a fascinating story about music conductor Carlos Kleiber concentrating so intently during a performance of Strauss's *Der Rosenkavalier* that he didn't notice an earthquake rattling giant chandeliers at the La Scala Opera House in Italy.

The ability to concentrate (including your length of attention span and intensity of focus) varies from person to person and for different activities. Differences in concentration levels exist between teammates on every curling team, but some events, such as a Canadian or World Championship, can distract even those with a high ability to concentrate. With experience and practice, though, everyone can learn to concentrate more effectively and recover more quickly from distractions. Young curlers are especially prone to distractions because they are still learning appropriate concentration and are more influenced by diversions. For coaches of junior teams, helping players understand the importance of concentration and developing strategies to cope with lapses in attention is time well spent. Successful curlers know how to maintain their focus and successful teams develop plans to manage the many and varied distractions that exist in a competitive environment.

Affirmations, or self-talk, chosen by you (or with help from your teammates or coach) and appropriately used, support how you want to see yourself ("I'm a good shot-maker.") or reinforce a goal you've set for yourself in practice or a game ("I can make this freeze."). To be successful, affirmations must be positive ("I can" / "I will"), in the present tense ("now") and personal ("I"). Most important, you must believe what you are saying, even if you resist at first. The purpose of self-talk is to counter negative thinking and challenge self-doubt. This will give you greater confidence, which in turn contributes positively to your performance. Does this work? Absolutely. Try remembering a time when you were afraid you'd miss a shot and, then, a time when you sat in the hack and just knew you'd be successful. Odds are that you missed your first shot and made your second one.

After executing a perfect double against Shannon Kleibrink in the final game of the 1997 Olympic Trials, Sandra Schmirler described sitting in the hack "knowing" she would make the shot. Her powerful self-talk led to one of the most memorable shots in Canadian curling. My teammate Joyce McKee also made an unforgettable comment to me very early in my competitive career. Joyce told me that one of the things that set me apart from many other curlers was that I never missed a crucial shot. Young and impressionable, I bought into her message completely because it was consistent with how I wanted to see myself. I stashed her comment in my "library" of messages, putting it to good use for many years whenever a "must make" situation arose. This single positive remark, offered at a time when I was growing as a curler and most receptive, probably did as much to define my curling career as all my on-ice practice.

These three tools—imagery, concentration, and self-talk—will help you define your skill as a curler.

IMAGERY

Imagery is the process of receiving and retaining information from the external environment through our senses. We also generate images from memory. Together, they give us an archive of pictures, which are powerful tools made up of real and imagined events.

Imagery is similar but not identical to mental rehearsal and visualization. The process of mental rehearsal involves creating a complete task (like playing an entire game or end) in your mind, while visualization involves only the visual component of a task (like seeing your rock slide into the four foot and stop).

Imagery differs in that it relies on all relevant senses. For example, if you want to use imagery to deliver a rock, you need to create a complete experience, including detailed visual pictures of your delivery from the front, back, and side. You should feel every aspect of your delivery kines-thetically—your thrust from the hack, the feeling in your legs, arms, and hands, and the cold smoothness of the rock handle gripped gently in your fingers. Hearing the rumble of the rock and feeling its speed as it moves along the ice enhances your overall image.

People have imagery preferences: some are better at "seeing" and others are better at "feeling" the experience. Your goal should be to improve in all areas of imagery, but if that proves difficult, work regularly with your strongest sense and definitely rely on it in competition. When you are imaging a specific technique (such as the release of a rock and its rotation), make sure you're using the correct form and not rehearsing an error.

The value of imagery as a relaxation tool is discussed in the Imagery section of the previous chapter. If you practise imagery systematically for even a few minutes on a regular basis, you can also use it to work on a specific skill, review past performances to correct mistakes and reinforce what worked, and rehearse strategies for modelling your behaviour before, during, and after a game.

Practising Skill-specific Imagery

To work on specific skills, follow these five steps:

1. Make a list of the skills/techniques you want to review (for example, your delivery broken down into its components; brushing).

2. Check the list with your coach.

3. For each skill/technique, verbalize your image of it to your coach or teammates to be sure it's technically correct.

4. Rehearse the images regularly and rate them from 1 to 5 (1 = very poor; 3 = average; 5 = excellent) on a log, like the example log provided on page 56. You should rehearse at home and during on-ice practices. It is important that you be able to recall these images just prior to a game and on the ice, between shots, or during breaks.

5. Apply all the relevant senses as vividly as you can and try to feel the correct movement in each component. **Taking time to relax before each session will help you develop your imaging experience.**

Use the log included here to help you develop imagery with your delivery (a similar log can be used with skills like brushing and timing rocks). Once you've imaged each component successfully, you can then combine them to produce an accurate image of your entire delivery, including smoothness of execution and accurate timing. Your imaging should simulate what you will do on the ice. The basic elements of delivering a rock are noted on the log, but you may want to add other items that are unique to your execution. If, for example, this was David Nedohin's imaging log, he would want to add the more pronounced angle in his throwing arm that he uses when he slides out and his unique way of taking his rock back. Each time you mentally rehearse an element of your delivery, give it a clarity rating in the space provided.

Imaging elements of your delivery correctly will make your delivery more consistent and produce more accurate shots. You can also use imaging with specific elements like stance or slide to help correct errors. Many curlers develop tendencies that result in consistent mistakes, which they must learn to recognize and fix. **The technical work of fixing a problem like incorrect alignment or early rock release is assisted when clear imaging is involved in the correction.**

When using the log, if your ratings of a specific element in your delivery are low, this weaker image is a sign of a potential problem. Trying another imaging technique can help correct the problem. For example, if visualizing your release lacks clarity, try a cue word like "now" to time your release at the same time you try to "feel" your release kinesthetically. Remember, imaging relies on all senses and when one, like visualization, is not working, switch to another, like trying to "feel" the correct technique. Your rock release should improve along with the imaging ratings in your log.

A few years ago, a promising young figure skater was referred to me because she fell consistently when she was attempting a double axel. First, we verbally broke the axel down into all its elements, which I had her visualize. It turned out she could picture all the elements but one, so we focused on this weak link with appropriate words and had her describe it kinesthetically. Because her visualization was weak, using words and "feeling" the movement helped to strengthen her image. Once I was satisfied that she could describe and feel the element correctly, it was time to try a double axel. Her effort was awkward but she did not fall, and as her confidence returned so did the double axel.

SKILL SPECIFIC IMAGERY LOG

SKILL: *Delivery*

Exercise Rating of Image Clarity: 1–5 (1 = very poor; 3 = average; 5 = excellent)

ELEMENTS	IMAGERY REHEARSAL									
	1	2	3	4	5	6	7	8	9	10
Stance										
- Front										
- Back										
- Side										
Rock Handle										
- Grip										
- Angle										
Rock Alignment										
Rock Motion Back										
Rock Motion Forward										
Slide										
- Posture										
- Rock Position										
- Brush Position										
- Sliding Foot Position										
- Hand Position										
Release										
Timing (Entire Delivery)										
Balance (Entire Delivery)										
Other Elements										

+ To improve your imagery skill, have your delivery videotaped. Play a sequence. Stop, close your eyes, and image what you just saw on the video.

+ Make sure you are imaging the correct elements of your delivery. If you or your coach identify an error on the tape, do more than just discuss it with your coach. Take time to close your eyes, image the correct delivery, and talk yourself through the correction before you attempt the actual delivery.

Reviewing Past Performances

Missing a shot, especially at a crucial time, is a painful experience. It is tempting to avoid looking back at it because it is so unpleasant. But even though you can't take back a missed shot, you can review it later to determine why it happened and how to prevent doing it again. On the other hand, making an important shot that turns an end or game around is one of the most exhilarating moments in curling. These are the shots that you willingly relive, not only because they're good memories but also to reinforce what worked for you.

A log like the one found here can help you use past events to strengthen your successes and correct your mistakes. List an event, your error or success at the event, and the reason for it. (Sometimes, you will recognize the mistake yourself immediately after it happens. Your coach or a teammate may also have noticed something you did wrong.) Then, each time you mentally correct an error or reinforce a good performance, rate your imaging from 1 to 5. To get you started, an example is provided in each section.

MENTALLY REHEARSING PAST PERFORMANCES LOG

Imagery Rating: 1–5 (1 = very poor; 3 = average; 5 = excellent)

ERROR CORRECTION

	EVENT	ERROR	REASON	CORRECTIVE IMAGING			
				1	2	3	4
1	*Ninth End Super League Final*	*Threw narrow and rubbed guard*	*Started the rock*				
2							
3							
4							
5							

GOOD PERFORMANCE

	EVENT	GOOD EXECUTION	REASON	REINFORCING IMAGING			
				1	2	3	4
1	*Tenth End Final Abbotsford 'Spiel*	*Perfect draw around guard to front of tee line*	*Good alignment and good rock release*				
2							
3							
4							
5							

Rehearsing Strategies for Future Competition

There are a number of rehearsal strategies you can use to help you prepare for competition. Actually visiting a future competition site to play a practice game or to work out on the ice as a team is one strategy. When a site visit, like a first trip to the Scottie or the Brier, is not possible, teams often consult curlers who have played at that level and are willing to share their experiences.

Mentally rehearsing the circumstances you expect to encounter leading up to, during, and after a competition is another good strategy. Competitive teams usually have a pre-game routine that they plan and rehearse before a competition. This is particularly valuable because smart curling is as much about how you prepare before you step on the ice as what you do in the game. Anticipating and rehearsing what might happen during a game and how you'll respond is another effective strategy. This takes away some of the surprise and subsequent stress associated with incidents like a pick, a broomed rock, or a hogline violation. Finally, planning and rehearsing what you do after a game—win or lose—helps you plan for the next one.

The rehearsal log found here can help you prepare for competition. Although the imagery used in this exercise is more general than the imagery you used to work on your delivery, you still want to capture the rehearsal as fully as possible, using all relevant senses. For example, suppose you and your teammates want to rehearse the environment you'll encounter just before the first game of a major competition. Assume that your team has made a pre-event site visit so everyone knows the general layout. Work with your teammates to prepare a shared list of items (which can be added to at any time) that will help you rehearse—individually—what will happen before, during, and after your game. (Some items are included on the log as examples.)

Start your rehearsal by mentally entering the building and imaging the presence of fans, family, and friends, other teams, the ice surface, and so on. Experience the energy and excitement you'll feel when you witness the buzz of activity and hear the hum of conversations around you. As you deliberately build your excitement in this rehearsal, imagine yourself taking one or two deep breaths and telling yourself that you're relaxed and ready to curl. Then move on to imagine what will happen during and after the game.

Each time you mentally rehearse an item from the list, give yourself a rating (from 1 to 5) in the space provided on the log. The imagery for this log does not have to be as vivid as those you develop for skill and to review past performance. You and your teammates can develop the list to make sure that all important items, like the presence of fans, are covered. You can then rehearse these on your own and discuss them with your teammates prior to each major competition. Obviously, though, the clearer your images are, the better your preparation.

FUTURE COMPETITION LOG

Name of Competition: _____

Rehearsal Quality: 1–5 (1 = very poor; 3 = average; 5 = excellent)

	ITEMS TO REHEARSE	1	2	3	4	5	6	7
1	The Setting							
	- Entrance							
	- Fan area							
	- Ice							
	- Teammates							
	- Other teams							
	-							
	-							
	-							
	-							
2	The Game							
	- Good first end							
	- Poor first end							
	- Other ends							
	- Unpredictable circumstances							
	-							
	-							
	-							
	-							
3	After the Game							
	- Shake hands							
	- Locker room behaviour							
	- Discuss what to do next							
	-							
	-							
	-							
	-							

NUMBER

CONCENTRATION

The ability to concentrate is crucial to performing well. If you can focus your attention on an immediate, relevant task, like hitting the broom, and not be sidetracked by an inappropriate stimulus, like someone shouting on an adjacent sheet of ice, or an internal distraction, like worrying about missing, you're more likely to perform it successfully. Concentration involves not being diverted by irrelevant stimuli, being in the present (not the past or the future), and, perhaps most important, having the ability to quickly refocus when concentration is lost. Focusing intensely and appropriately for the required length of time and refocusing quickly when necessary are what some psychologists call "selective awareness."

Sport psychologist Robert Nideffer[10] identified four kinds of concentration:

- Broad – demands attention to multiple stimuli, like following the path, speed, and rotation of a rock down the ice

- Narrow – requires a focus on one thing; concentrating on the skip's broom before delivering a rock is an obvious example

- External – refers to stimuli outside yourself, like ice temperature, crowd noise, or rock position

- Internal – relates to your internal state physically, cognitively, and emotionally

Placed on a quadrant, these four areas cover the major attentional demands in curling. The following diagram shows how these areas can either be helpful or distracting, depending on when and how each is applied. For example, you use broad internal and external concentration when you look at rocks in the house and their positions (external) and when you contemplate different strategy options (internal). When you can see in your mind what the house will look like after a shot, your concentration is broad–internal.

CONCENTRATION

	BROAD	
	POSITIVE	POSITIVE
	Scanning the house—the number of rocks and their positions	Visualizing what the house will look like after a shot is completed
	NEGATIVE	NEGATIVE
	Crowd noise	Worring about playing poorly and what others will think
EXTERNAL		**INTERNAL**
	POSITIVE	POSITIVE
	Concentrating on the broom prior to delivery	"Feeling" the weight you want to throw
	NEGATIVE	NEGATIVE
	Your rock is removed from play	Afraid to throw your in-turn
	NARROW	

Nideffer also set out several principles that are associated with concentration, all of which are relevant to curling.

- Athletes should be capable of applying all four kinds of concentration: broad, narrow, external, and internal.

- Different situations call for different kinds of concentration. Scanning rocks in the house and anticipating what changes will result from a big-weight shot compared with a tap back requires both a broad internal and a broad external focus. Sitting in the hack concentrating solely on the brush at the far end of the ice, however, requires a narrow external focus. Curlers need to be able to use all four areas of focus and shift to different quadrants as circumstances change.

- Under ideal conditions, athletes will likely achieve the concentration that is demanded of them. In curling, however, conditions are seldom ideal because they are determined more by shots made or missed and by how curlers react to the fickleness of the game. What separates curlers who excel from good curlers is their ability to make the most of less-than-ideal circumstances. As a friend of mine who is a bridge player once remarked, "Success in bridge is not so much an ability to play a good hand as it is to get the most out of a poorly dealt hand." The same applies to curling.

- Just as athletes have different abilities due to their different biological and genetic makeup, they also have different tendencies in terms of concentration. Athletes who practise their weaker areas of concentration can improve in those areas, but their natural preference will still dominate. It is tempting to think that these skills should be considered when team positions are being decided. Someone whose focus is more narrow than broad, for example, would likely not enjoy skipping.

- As activation (arousal) increases beyond an optimal level, athletes typically display their more dominant tendency. This is why, under high pressure, some focus narrowly while others seem "scattered" in their thinking. For example, if shot selection is crucial, a curler with a naturally narrow focus may overlook alternative shots, while the athlete with scattered thinking will be hard pressed to attend to the task at hand—the eventual shot choice.

- "Choking" is an involuntary narrowing of

internal concentration that contributes to poor performance. In a high pressure situation, like a draw to the four foot against four opposition stones in the eighth end of an important game, the curler who handles pressure well will take a deep breath, remember important delivery cues and visualize the completed shot. The involuntary narrowing of attention that produces choking occurs when a curler, without being aware (involuntary), becomes anxious and worries more about missing (narrowing) than visualizing a successful outcome.

- Changes in physiological activation affect an athlete's concentration. This means that deliberately increasing or decreasing activation levels, for example, deep breathing to relax before throwing a rock, can improve concentration.

- Concentration, in turn, can be used to change physiological activation. Focusing on something pleasant, taking a brief "time out" and refocusing can help to control activation before an important shot.

Tips for Improving Concentration

Try the following strategies to improve your concentration skills in different areas:

Broad External

- Use a game board (I've also seen houses set up with coffee cups), either on your own or with your teammates, to look at various strategy situations and talk through the situations and shot choices. The next time you face something similar on the ice, chances are you'll remember your earlier review.

- Practise looking at an object while you remain generally aware of surrounding objects. Which objects distract you? Your goal is to remain focused on the main object. Gradually make this drill part of your on-ice practice.

Broad Internal

- See how much you can recall about a recent practice session or game. You can do this alone and with your teammates.

Narrow External

- Calculate how much time you need, on average, to deliver a rock once you're in position in the hack. At practice, have a teammate time your ability to focus on the broom without becoming distracted by something on the ice or having your mind wander. The stopwatch starts when you signal you're ready to concentrate on the broom. It stops when you signal you've lost your concentration. Your goal is to maintain concentration for the time you need to deliver your rock.

- Choose an object and try to concentrate on it for thirty seconds. Record the number of times you are distracted. Each time you concentrate on the object add a distraction. Your goal is to be able to concentrate on the object despite multiple distractions.

Narrow Internal

- Use physical strategies, like relaxation and deep breathing, and cognitive approaches, like self-talk, to strengthen your ability to focus internally. When you become more aware of your thoughts and emotions, you can focus more effectively on managing them.

- Select a thought and try to hold it for fifteen seconds. Time yourself to see how long it is before you lose the thought. Your goal is to gradually increase the length of time you can hold a single thought.

More on Distractions

Because distractions are an inevitable part of curling, you can't avoid them completely. The most effective coping strategy is to learn to recognize a distraction as quickly as possible and then apply an effective technique to refocus. Self-talk and thought stopping and replacement are the most effective ways to stop and replace distractions with more appropriate concentration.

The following exercise lists a number of external and internal distractions. Space is left for you to add others. Beside each distraction, write a statement you could use to refocus. Self-talk is the most effective technique because most distractions occur on ice and you don't have time to implement others.

Early in my career, I gained unforgettable experience on the impact that distractions—positive and negative—can have on curling performance. I was coach of the Linda Moore team for the 1988 Calgary Olympics. Linda, Lindsay Sparkes, Debbie Jones, Penny Ryan, Patti Vande, and I had worked together for nearly a year and knew each other well by the time the competition began in mid-February. In 1987, the Olympic Trials (where the Moore team earned the right to

DISTRACTIONS EXERCISE

EXTERNAL	REFOCUSING STATEMENT
Comment from an opponent	*"He can't get to me."*
Noise makes it hard to hear your skip	
Family/friends at the game	
Delay in starting your game	
Having a driver for the first time	
A rock that "picks"	

INTERNAL	REFOCUSING STATEMENT
Physical	
"I'm tired. I didn't sleep well."	*"I have energy for this game and will rest later."*
Thoughts	
"We haven't beaten this team this year."	*"We're due."*
Feelings	
"I'm worried about playing poorly."	*"One shot at a time and the outcome will take care of itself."*

represent Canada) were held in Max Bell Arena in Calgary. Since we were familiar with the facility, we thought we were prepared for any potential distractions. We missed one.

In our planning we discussed how to cope with large crowds of knowledgeable, supportive Canadian fans. Instead, we got something very different. Early in the competition reports claimed that Max Bell Arena was sold out. For most of the round-robin games, Linda Moore and Ed Lukowich played before sparse crowds. Then, just as the teams became accustomed to that level of fan support, the ticket problem was solved. Suddenly, Max Bell Arena was filled to capacity with enthusiastic curling fans. We had to deal with a distraction that had changed suddenly and significantly. The teams coped well. Ed Lukowich, John Ferguson, Neil Houston, and Brent Syme earned a bronze medal. I will never forget the bedlam that resulted when Linda Moore made her final shot to defeat Sweden's Elisabeth Hogstrom 7–5 to claim the gold medal for Canada.

Less than two months later I was off to Glasgow, Scotland, for the World Championships with a team I did not know nearly as well as the Moore team. This was the first exposure to international competition outside Canada for 1988 Scott Tournament of Hearts Champions Heather Houston, Lorraine Lang, Diane Adams, Tracy Kennedy, Gloria Taylor, and me.

Prior to the event, I had been warned that the competition would be different from what we were used to in Canada. Event planning, I was told, would be decent but not as thorough, and crowd support would not be as impartial compared with Canadian championships. Fans sided with the underdog, which usually meant anyone but Canada.

Advice like this, while helpful, is not the same as experiencing these distractions firsthand. In Glasgow, officials listened politely to questions from the Canadian team about the details of competition but then either ignored requests or granted them only after keeping us in limbo for extended periods. For example, our request to match rocks prior to the playoffs was first denied then finally granted so late into the evening that the team returned to its hotel at a very late hour. Fan appreciation for Canadian shots was lukewarm at best and much more enthusiastic for their opponents. The hurdles that the Canadians encountered in Glasgow were varied and numerous.

The team persevered, eventually losing the championship final to Germany's Andrea Schopp. While the loss was a bitter one (Canadian curlers don't like finishing second), the experience was valuable. The next year, in Milwaukee, Heather Houston skipped the same team to a gold medal over Norway's Dordi Nordby. Andrea Schopp finished third, losing the semi-final game 8–5 to Houston.

SELF-TALK

Applied to sport, affirmations, or self-talk, are words or statements that enhance performance when used appropriately. Sport psychologist and former gymnast Steven Ungerleider[11] describes these messages as a personal "pep-talk." Affirmations can be technical ("sliding foot flat"), motivational ("We've been here before. We can win."), general ("We're ready!"), individual and private ("I am the best lead here."), or team focused ("We're on a roll."). The list is endless but, as you know from Chapter 1, the best self-talk uses simple, positive language, is in the present tense, and, most important, is personally meaningful and not forced.

Ungerleider described how champion tennis player Pete Sampras used self-talk as an essential ingredient to his remarkable career. "Sampras . . . tended to let anger trap him . . . and he allowed it to lead to negative tension on the court. To combat this tendency, Sampras learned to say positive things to himself such as 'I need to get out of this mind-set' or 'I need to stay focused on the present and prepare for the next point.'"[12] By using this approach, Sampras became less easily distracted and more attentive to his game. Perhaps the most successful player of the modern age, Sampras had won sixty-four singles titles by the time he retired in 2003, including two Australian and four US Open titles and seven Wimbledon Championships. His website notes that his skill, determination, and consistency were admired by fans and fellow players alike, but his success was the result of more than skill. His determination and consistency were due to his well-developed psychological abilities, particularly his reliance on positive affirmations. What worked for Pete Sampras will work for you.

The benefits of positive self-talk accrue with time. Like other skills, they need to be practised until they are part of your "belief system"—the component that affects the way you think and, therefore, how you perform. Compared to techniques like relaxation or concentration, self-talk is more individualized and personal. Affirmations are **your** words, selected and "tailor-made" for you, and if you accept that they work, they will. If you find it difficult to accept your affirmations and your resistance doesn't diminish with practise, a deeper seated belief system may be interfering with the changes you want to implement. (If this happens, you should work with a sport psychologist to get a better understanding of what lies behind your resistance.)

Three types of affirmation—technical, motivational, and general—encompass the five areas identified earlier in this section and they all contribute to performance.

- Technical affirmations help improve your on-ice skills. For example, phrases such as "wrist straight" or "slow and smooth" can help keep your delivery consistent.

- Motivational affirmations keep you stimulated. You can use the same statement repeatedly, especially when it's associated with prior success. If a statement begins to lose its power for you, find a new one. Statements can also be used to adjust motivation. I used the statement "How will I feel if I continue to play lousy and we lose?" to motivate me when I found myself becoming complacent. If you find yourself overly motivated, words like "calm" or "relax" can reduce your motivation to an acceptable level.

- General affirmations can be used to correct problems. If, for example, you have a problem judging weight, find a word that reminds you how to correct the problem and say it to yourself as you follow a rock down the ice.

Affirmations also help you maintain your confidence. Clearly, positive results give you confidence, but the potential for failure is always present and even the best athletes have "off days." Self-talk that reminds you of past successes helps to soften disappointment and gets you ready for the next challenge.

How to Develop Personal Affirmations

First, identify technical problems you know of that affect your delivery or your motivation. Then, on the following log, list words and statements that you think will help you improve technically and keep you motivated and confident. Your coach and teammates can help, but the final choice must be yours. As you rehearse these words and statements, become aware of their effect on you and make every effort to make them meaningful. Add new words as they occur to you and replace those that are no longer effective.

SOME FINAL THOUGHTS ON IMAGERY, CONCENTRATION, AND SELF-TALK

We apply imagery, concentration, and self-talk in many of the everyday things we do. People like music conductor Carlos Kleiber and tennis great Pete Sampras added these qualities to their already formidable talents to achieve success in their remarkable careers. You can become a better curler by learning and, then, systematically practising and applying these techniques until they become as familiar as

AFFIRMATIONS LOG

1. TECHNICAL: e.g., "Shoulders square."

_____	_____
_____	_____
_____	_____
_____	_____
_____	_____
_____	_____
_____	_____

2. MOTIVATIONAL: e.g., "We own the ice."

_____	_____
_____	_____
_____	_____
_____	_____
_____	_____
_____	_____
_____	_____

3. GENERAL: e.g., "Think positive."

_____

_____

_____

_____

_____

_____

_____

_____

an on-ice practice routine. Obviously, not everyone becomes a Glenn Howard or a Kelly Scott, but any curler can improve and therefore find greater personal satisfaction in competing. One thing is clear: the Howards and Scotts use these techniques because they work.

The next chapter describes effective communication, cohesive teamwork, and productive goal setting. They contribute mental toughness and improve team dynamics. Added to your technical and tactical skills, they increase your chance of competitive success.

Mental Toughness and Team Dynamics

Successful curling teams have players who are skilled at all four positions. Curlers who excel have more than just shot-making ability, though. They have other qualities that add to their skill and help them achieve at a high level when game challenges are the greatest and stakes are the highest. All skilled curlers can make the same shots, but the reason that some make their shots more consistently than others is often attributed to mental toughness.

According to sport psychologist James Loehr, mentally tough athletes are:

- emotionally flexible (they handle the range of emotions that occurs in competition)

- responsive (they remain involved under pressure instead of withdrawing emotionally to protect themselves from potential disappointment)

- strong (they make a great emotional commitment under pressure)

- resilient (they recover quickly from disappointment).[13]

Because team members have different personalities, they will possess these qualities in varying degrees. The curler who gets over a loss quickly, for example, can often help a teammate who is slower to recover. Think about the last time you were still fuming about a loss when a teammate contributed a "mood saver" by saying something funny. The best teams have players with all four qualities that, collectively, provide the ingredients they need for a mentally tough team.

You and your teammates can develop the mental toughness you need to compete more successfully. It just takes commitment—to effective communication, cohesive teamwork, and productive goal setting.

> "Success is not final, failure is not fatal; it is the courage to continue that counts."
> *Winston Churchill*

EFFECTIVE COMMUNICATION

Communication involves sending a message to someone with the intention of having an effect. We rely primarily on verbal messages to convey information (like discussing which shot to play) and on non-verbal messages, such as gesture, tone of voice, eye contact, space, body language, or even saying nothing, to convey emotion. Much of our communication is a combination of verbal and non-verbal messages. For instance, saying "good shot" sends a message, but it is the enthusiasm in your tone of voice and the pat on the back that conveys your true satisfaction with a teammate's effort.

When you are the communicator, you rely on public expressions, like words and gestures, to send your message to another person or group. Your message has an effect on your recipient, who then responds with words and non-verbal behaviour. When these actions and words are consistent in terms of your intentions and your message's effect on your recipient, there is effective communication. When the curler who made the good shot says "thanks" to his teammate who patted him on the back, both would likely agree that their communication was comfortable and congruent.

The communication process is relatively simple, but the act of communicating can be complex, as this chart illustrates:

SKIP'S INTENTIONS --->
(private)

*Convey appreciation
for a good shot*

or

*Improve confidence in a
teammate who is not
having a good game*

or

*Mask frustration over the
teammate's less than
stellar play to that point*

SKIP'S BEHAVIOURS --->
(public)

*Says "Good shot."
Pats teammate on the back.*

EFFECT ON TEAMMATE
(private)

*I made a good shot.
Now I'll play better.*

or

*Why did he say that now
when he didn't say it for
the other shot I made?*

TEAMMATE'S INTENTION
(private)

I'm not sure what he means, but I'll acknowledge what he said.

**TEAMMATE'S <---
BEHAVIOUR**
(public)

Says "Thanks."

EFFECT ON SKIP <---
(private)

*Good. He heard me.
I hope things go
better now.*

⟶

End of Communication Sequence

Although this exchange was congenial, the skip and his teammate didn't know the exact intentions or the effects of it on each other. Over time, as you and your teammates get to know each other well, you should begin to trust their public messages and assume that the private motives behind exchanges are in everyone's best interest. If that doesn't happen, there is a definite potential for problems on your team.

Problems result when intentions, effects, and verbal and non-verbal actions are not complementary or when something is blocking them. Many things can hinder communication. Interference can be environmental. Think of the last time you couldn't hear your skip because there was so much shouting on an adjacent sheet of ice. Interference can also be personal and internal. Attitudes, biases, worries, and other emotions enter into our communication with others and sometimes get in the way of what is being transmitted. Verbal and non-verbal exchanges are also occasionally mixed, either deliberately or inadvertently. When that happens, the listener invariably places greater trust in the non-verbal message. If the skip in the previous example had said "good shot" in a sarcastic way with no pat on the back, his teammate would have had no trouble discerning, accurately, that the skip was still frustrated with his earlier misses.

Effective communication can take a team a long way in competition but only if everyone on the team makes an honest and deliberate effort to understand and be understood (more on problems with teammates in the next chapter). The best teams develop consistent, precise technical language that they use on ice to communicate rock movement and rotation, weight, and line to ensure that a thrown rock finishes as accurately as possible. A simple word like "room" tells sweepers that a rock has sufficient room (at that moment) to get by a guard and they can concentrate mainly on weight. The brusher who replies "six" is telling the skip, based on the team's system for judging weight, where the rock is expected to finish.

Dealing with Disagreements

Most competitive teams have plans for technical communication, but many don't have plans to deal with personal misunderstandings that arise during the course of a season. Between October and March, teammates spend a lot of time—some of it high stress—at the rink, travelling, and in hotel rooms. This togetherness can become stifling unless teammates give each other space and "time outs" (time alone and/or with family or friends) or, depending on circumstances, even a brief break from competition. The curler who misses a weekend bonspiel to attend to career, family, or school demands often returns to the ice with renewed enthusiasm, and her teammates are happy to have her back. Teams and individuals differ. Before developing a seasonal schedule and plans for each competition, you and your teammates should discuss your individual needs so expectations are understood and agreed upon. That way, a teammate's occasional need for privacy won't be misinterpreted as avoidance. (Tips for reducing family-, school-, or career-related stress are given in the Time Management section of Chapter 1.)

The passion of competition carries a great range and intensity of emotions that extend from excitement over an impending shot, to frustration and disappointment when things don't work out, to joy and the release of tension that accompanies last-rock success. Yet emotions, whether expressed or suppressed, can cause misunderstanding and interfere with a team's communication. In one case I know, a team member had chosen to express her emotions by swearing. The more stressful the situation, the stronger and more frequent her profanity became and, in time, this wore on her teammates. The problem wasn't so much her swearing—it was more that her outbursts signaled her lack of mental discipline.

Suppressed emotions are equally problematic. If they go on for some time, they eventually find an outlet, usually inappropriate and poorly timed. Dealing with curling business, like strategy and practice times, is easy. Interpersonal communication is far more sensitive. In my experience, many curlers are reluctant to raise interpersonal concerns with teammates because they either don't want to risk hurting feelings or fear the fallout that might result.

A seasonal plan should include a strategy to deal with personal issues and misunderstandings. If you and your teammates are honest with each other, your team's chances of success will improve because your focus will be on curling, not on relationships. Your team's strategy can take various forms. The members of the Randy Ferbey foursome, for example, are quite direct with each other and, although other curlers might find their intensity jarring, this strategy works for them. In contrast, Glenn Howard's 2007 Brier and World Champions are much calmer in their exchanges with each other. I've been involved with teams who were not comfortable disagreeing strongly and publicly. Instead, their strategy was to set aside time at the end of each day to debrief and consider any issues that might have developed. Teammates could concentrate on the game and set aside an immediate problem, knowing it would be raised later, and issues could be resolved while they were still minor. This is a case where a coach can be invaluable as a mediator and a problem solver for the entire team or for individual members.

To improve your curling success, you and your teammates must commit to sharing information honestly, solving your problems co-operatively, and minimizing your misunderstandings. A few basic tips to lower the potential for tension in your interpersonal exchanges are outlined next. (If they don't help, involve your coach. If an interpersonal problem becomes serious, consult a sport psychologist.)

Tips for Decreasing Tension among Teammates

Sender's skills (talking) are most effective when they provide information. Attacks and putdowns force the other person to become defensive. You can do two things to keep the intensity between you and the other person more manageable:

1. Focus on the behaviour, not the person. For example, try saying:

- "What time did you get on that rock?" vs. "You must have gotten the wrong time."

- "Jim, you are doing most of the talking." vs. "Jim, you are a know-it-all."

2. Describe your feelings rather than accuse the other person. For example, try saying:

- "I'm too upset to talk right now." vs. "Leave me alone."

- "It irritates me when you interrupt me." vs. "Geez, you're rude."

To improve your receiving (listening) skills, try these two techniques:

1. Check the meaning of what was said by paraphrasing it back to the sender. If your paraphrase is accurate, the sender will feel understood. If it is inaccurate, you have an opportunity to clarify it. For example:

   - **Sender:** "I think we should look at a different game plan for our next game. The last time we played them, we were too defensive."
     Receiver: "It sounds like you think we should be more aggressive."

     or

   - **Sender:** "Our third just bad-mouthed our skip to me."
     Receiver: "Are you saying she is trying to undermine her?"

Introducing replies with phrases like "Do you mean ...?" or "It sounds like ..." or "Are you saying ...?" and then giving an example is a good way to be sure that you and the sender have a mutual understanding of an exchange. Too often problems arise because the sender assumes that the recipient understands the purpose of his message in the same way that he does, but this is not always the case. Paraphrasing helps ensure that the listener understands the message in the way that the receiver intended.

2. Check the emotional element of what was said by making a comment that also has an emotional element. If you guess the feeling correctly, your listener will feel understood. If you are incorrect, you have an opportunity to clarify the message. For example:

- **Sender:** Sits quietly in a corner looking unhappy.
  Receiver: "You look annoyed."

or

- **Sender:** "Let's leave."
  Receiver: "You sound upset. Let's go."

Dealing with Conflict

Disagreements are not pleasant, and people react to them in different ways.

Avoidance: When faced with conflict, some people choose not to participate. This can be an acceptable reaction for a minor issue, but if the conflict continues or is significant (such as consistently finding fault with a teammate), it is not a preferred option—first, because the problem is not being addressed and, second, because the person under attack risks being seen as lacking in mental courage. In my experience, some very determined competitors are mistakenly viewed as lacking mental toughness simply because they refuse to confront people who try to intimidate them. It is possible to bring mental toughness to a curling game but be seen as lacking mental toughness simply due to a distaste for personal confrontation. Although it can be difficult, curlers who dislike conflict should be prepared to stand up for themselves.

> "Be who you are and say what you feel,
> because those who mind don't matter
> and those who matter don't mind."
>
> *Dr. Seuss*

Denial: This is another example of withdrawal. I've seen curlers dismiss a teammate's unsportsmanlike behaviour by saying, "Oh, that's just the way he is." Denial is unhelpful because it allows problematic behaviour to continue and promotes a double standard (with the potential for resentment) because one curler's behaviour is tolerated but that of others is not. Denying that frustrating behaviour exists can be as hard on teammates as the stress that results from simply deciding to tackle the problem.

Accommodation: Giving in is an acceptable strategy when the issue is either minor or not important to you. Sometimes, it's better to let a matter rest than risk turning it into something major. How do you know if accommodation is the right choice? If you're mildly irritated, let the matter rest, at least for the present. If you have strong feelings or if an issue persists, develop a plan to deal with it by consulting with your coach, a family member, or a trusted friend. Then, follow through.

Compromise and Collaboration: This is the preferred option when both people in a disagreement are willing to make concessions. The result is a negotiated resolution to a problem that involves some give-and-take on both sides.

Switching positions is one of the most sensitive issues a team may have to deal with. For example, there was potential for serious disagreement when a junior skip I know moved to third at her coach's initiative. Less than tactful members of the curling community made comments to her like "Oh, I see you've been demoted." The new skip, previously the third, also showed initial insensitivity in her excitement over her new-found prominence. The coach resolved the situation by stressing to his players the importance of all their roles. In a private conversation, I reminded the new third that Olympic Champion Sandra Schmirler had gained valuable experience as a third before becoming a superb skip. Eventually, the gossip stopped (winning important games helped), and the team went on to a solid season. Success was achieved, in a large part, through compromise: the third accepted her new role and the skip respected the third for her decision.

Confrontation: There are times when it is necessary to raise a problem and confront its source. On ice, when team members disagree over what shot to play, someone (usually the skip) confronts the uncertainty and makes a decision. Off ice, confronting a teammate may be much harder. You should plan it well and follow two basic rules: 1) if possible, confront your teammate without being aggressive and 2) have someone, such as your coach, mediate.

Aggression: Fortunately, this level of disagreement is rare in curling. Curling fans don't riot and on-ice penalties result from rule enforcement, not conflict between opposing curlers. However, an aggressor's intention in any disagreement is to win the argument. Aggressors have neither a concern for others nor a desire to compromise; they simply want to get their way, regardless of the cost. Although aggressors may win, bad feelings often result. Aggressive curlers usually don't remain on a seriously competitive team for long.

It is important to know how you and your teammates react to disagreements because it helps you get along better and have a greater understanding of your differences. Understanding each other and tolerating each other's differences contributes significantly to team cohesion. To keep communication lines open and manageable during potentially difficult discussions, try these strategies:

- Always listen carefully to what a teammate is saying. Half of good communication is listening.

- Before you reply to a comment, do a quick internal check to satisfy yourself that you heard the message. If you're not sure, ask for clarification. Then, mentally plan your reply. Too often, we respond quickly to what someone says without considering the impact of our response. People generally find pauses uncomfortable and want to rush to fill silences with words. A brief delay while you plan and get comfortable with your response is time well spent.

- Your reply should focus on the content of the message. The exception, of course, is when you want to clarify the emotional state of a teammate.

- Raise emotional or sensitive issues in a non-confrontational way. Remain calm and in control (which is hard to do sometimes). Showing that you are aware of what a teammate is experiencing can go a long way to getting issues into the open and resolved. Do things gradually. If you take your time, you remain in control.

People usually learn the strategies they use to manage conflict in childhood, and these seem to function automatically. We're typically unaware of how we act in conflict situations—we just do whatever seems to come naturally. But we do have a personal strategy, and, because it was learned, we can change it by learning new and more effective ways of managing conflict.

When you're involved in a conflict, there are two major issues you need to consider. The first is achieving your personal goals. You are in conflict because you have a goal that conflicts with another person's goal. How important your goal is to you—very important or of little importance—will affect how you react to the conflict. The second is keeping a good relationship with the other person. You may need to interact effectively with the other person in the future. How important the relationship is to you—very important or of little importance—will also determine how you react to the conflict.

How Do You React to Conflict?

Take the following test[14] to see how you tend to react to conflict situations. You and your teammates might want to compare your results because it will help you understand each other better when disagreements arise.

HOW YOU ACT IN CONFLICTS

Proverbs state traditional wisdom. The well-known proverbs listed below illustrate some of the different strategies that can be used to resolve conflicts. Read each proverb carefully and then use a number from 1 to 5 to indicate how typical it is of your actions in a conflict. When you're done, check the scoring guide.

PROVERBS/CONFLICT EXERCISE

Rating Scale:
5 = very typical; 4 = frequently typical; 3 = sometimes typical; 2 = seldom typical;
1 = never typical

_____ 1. It is easier to refrain than to retreat from a quarrel.

_____ 2. If you cannot make a person think as you do, make the person do as you think.

_____ 3. Soft words win hard hearts.

_____ 4. You scratch my back, I'll scratch yours.

_____ 5. Come now and let us reason together.

_____ 6. When two quarrel, the person who keeps silent first is the most praiseworthy.

_____ 7. Might overcomes right.

_____ 8. Smooth words make smooth ways.

_____ 9. Better half a loaf than no bread at all.

_____ 10. Truth lies in knowledge, not in majority opinion.

_____ 11. He who fights and runs away lives to fight another day.

_____ 12. He hath conquered well that hath made his enemies flee.

_____ 13. Kill your enemies with kindness.

_____ 14. A fair exchange brings no quarrel.

_____ 15. No person has the final answer, but every person has a piece to contribute.

_____ 16. Stay away from people who disagree with you.

_____ 17. Fields are won by those who believe in winning.

_____ 18. Kind words are worth much and cost little.

_____ 19. Tit for tat is fair play.

_____ 20. Only those who are willing to give up their monopoly on truth can ever profit from the truths that others hold.

_____ 21. Avoid quarrelsome people as they will only make your life miserable.

_____ 22. A person who will not flee will make others flee.

_____ 23. Soft words ensure harmony.

_____ 24. One gift for another makes good friends.

_____ 25. Bring your conflicts into the open and face them directly; only then will the best solution be discovered.

_____ 26. The best way of handling conflicts is to avoid them.

_____ 27. Put your foot down where you mean to stand.

_____ 28. Gentleness will triumph over anger.

_____ 29. Getting part of what you want is better than not getting anything at all.

_____ 30. Frankness, honesty, and trust will move mountains.

_____ 31. There is nothing so important you have to fight for it.

_____ 32. There are two kinds of people in the world: the winners and the losers.

_____ 33. When one hits you with a stone, hit him or her with a piece of cotton.

_____ 34. When both give in halfway, a fair settlement is achieved.

_____ 35. By digging and digging, the truth is discovered.

SCORING

Withdrawing	Forcing	Smoothing	Compromising	Confronting
_____ 1	_____ 2	_____ 3	_____ 4	_____ 5
_____ 6	_____ 7	_____ 8	_____ 9	_____ 10
_____ 11	_____ 12	_____ 13	_____ 14	_____ 15
_____ 16	_____ 17	_____ 18	_____ 19	_____ 20
_____ 21	_____ 22	_____ 23	_____ 24	_____ 25
_____ 26	_____ 27	_____ 28	_____ 29	_____ 30
_____ 31	_____ 32	_____ 33	_____ 34	_____ 35
_____ Total	_____ Total	_____ Total	_____ Total	_____ Total

How Do You Manage Conflict?

As noted earlier, how you act in, or manage, a conflict depends not only on how important your personal goals are to you but also on how important your relationship with the person you're in conflict with is to you. The scoring guide of the proverbs exercise identified the five styles of managing conflict that the proverbs demonstrate. These styles are described next.[15] Based on your test score, which style or styles do you tend to use?

- **Withdrawing** – If your score indicated this style, you tend to avoid issues that are causing conflict and those you are in conflict with. You are willing to give up personal goals and relationships because you believe that it is hopeless to try to resolve conflicts and it is easier to withdraw (physically and psychologically) from a conflict than to face it.

- **Forcing** – If this is your style, you tend to try to force opponents to accept your solution to a conflict by attacking, overpowering, overwhelming, and intimidating them. Your goals are highly important to you, and you try to achieve them at all costs. Relationships, however, are of minor importance as you are neither concerned with others' needs nor care if others like or accept you. You believe that conflicts are settled when someone wins, and you want to be that someone. Winning gives you a sense of pride and achievement; losing makes you feel like a failure.

- **Smoothing** – If you scored high in this category, relationships are far more important to you than your personal goals. You believe that conflicts should be avoided because people can't discuss conflicts without someone getting hurt and the relationship being damaged. You are willing to give up your personal goals to preserve the relationship because you want to be accepted and liked by others.

- **Compromising** – If your score indicated this style, you tend to be moderately concerned with both your personal goals and your relationships with others. You are willing to give up part of your goals and will work to persuade the other person in the conflict to do the same thing in order to find a common agreement that will benefit both of you.

- **Confronting** – If this is your style, you put a high value on your personal goals and on your relationships. You view a conflict as a problem to be solved and seek a solution that achieves your goals and those of the person you're in conflict with, and you are not satisfied until this is accomplished. You believe that confronting a problem can eventually reduce tension between two people and improve their relationship. Your goal is to maintain the relationship, and you are not satisfied until the tension and negative feelings are fully resolved.

Taking this test will help you think about how you are inclined to deal with conflict. Understanding not only how you react but also the strengths and limitations of your personal tendencies will help you consider adopting more varied approaches to dealing with conflict.

Improving How You Communicate with Teammates

Keeping a Journal

It has become common for elite athletes to keep a diary, and you may want to keep one too. You can use it as a record of your performance—both how you played and how you felt about your effort—and also as a log for any other topics you want to track. Your journal is private, of course, but you can discuss portions of it with your coach and teammates. You can also review it from time to time to relive the positive experiences that occur throughout the season and to make sure your concerns are addressed.

In addition to tracking your on-ice performance, you can use your journal to track how successfully you've used psychological tools. Are you using imagery, affirmations, thought management, and stress control regularly? How effective are they? Do you need to change how you apply a technique?

Finally, keeping a journal—on paper or on your computer—is therapeutic. It gives you a safe way to work out your feelings about your coach and teammates, instead of keeping them bottled up. Sometimes, just recording them is all you need to do. Other times, you may decide you need to talk to someone about how you feel. Your journal can be a valuable personal tool.

Team Meetings

Your team's plan for the season should include times for group discussions, with everyone contributing to the agenda. Busy curlers often rush to a practice or game and hurry away afterward. Team meetings over a snack at the rink before a game or in the lounge after the game, although not ideal because of the lack of privacy, are preferable to no meetings at all. If possible, arrange to meet at someone's home instead. Getting together just prior to a competition not only confirms plans but, positively structured, also helps to promote a feeling of teamwork. Debriefing after a positive experience is useful because everyone is in a good frame of mind and issues that have to be dealt with feel less negative when everyone is in a good mood. When an issue comes up that might compromise your team's goals, you all need to meet as quickly as possible, with your coach providing the leadership.

E-mails

Often, the quickest and best way to communicate with your team about administrative tasks is by e-mail. Practice, game, bonspiel, and playdown schedules, travel details, and budgeting can all be shared effectively via computer.

E-mail is not appropriate, however, for dealing with personal matters. Raising a concern with someone by e-mail (or by phone) is risky because it places you at a distance from the other person. Although you have control over your message, you have less ability to manage the other person's reaction to it, especially since sometimes we're more candid in our e-mail messages than perhaps we should be. When we talk directly with someone, most of us tend to choose our words more carefully. The rule of thumb is: e-mail for basic information and face-to-face personal discussions for everything else.

COHESIVE TEAMWORK

> "Coming together is a beginning,
> staying together is progress and
> working together is success."
>
> *Henry Ford*

Teamwork doesn't guarantee wins but success is unlikely without it. Over time, my work with coaches and athletes has taught me that no sport relies on teamwork the way that curling does.

When it comes to actual execution, curling is not much different from other team sports where athletes play specific positions that call for specialized skills and where success depends on how well each player performs. Quarterbacking a football team, pitching a baseball, or skipping a curling team all require skills specific to each position. What makes curling unique is the interdependence between the skip and those who play the other positions. Quarterbacks and pitchers rely on teammates to successfully complete a play, but they don't have to communicate directly to make this happen the way a skip does in a curling game. Similarly, receivers and fielders don't have the same input into strategy and play selection during a game that leads, seconds, and thirds do. This is the element of curling that demands cohesiveness between teammates unlike that in any other sport.

Although fifth players and coaches are now important positions in curling, their roles are different from most other sports where athletes are substituted in and out of lineups and the coach makes the key decisions. In curling, everyone on the team plans and consults beforehand but once four players step onto the ice, except for very structured time outs, their destiny is in their own hands. This is why teamwork is fundamental to curling. Clearly, for a team to be successful, teammates must communicate effectively and rely closely on each other. But being a cohesive team also involves being patient with teammates' different personalities and accepting the leadership that is inherent in the role of the skip but expressed in other forms by teammates. More than anything, teamwork requires curlers to set aside their individual egos for the good of the team.

This does not mean that you should be expected to have the same emotional commitments to your teammates as you have to your family and friends. (A curler who described her teammates as "sisters" caused me concern. The relationship is not the same.) Still, if you observe successful teams, their communication, their cohesion, and their personalities and leadership styles convey trust, respect, and a level of honesty found in other important relationships. This is one reason why some siblings work well together on the ice. Russ and Glenn Howard, Brier and World Champions in 1987 and 1993, are an example of a successful brother combination. Before them, the Richardson brothers (Ernie, Sam, and Wes), along with their cousin Arnold, claimed three Brier and World Championships in four years. The family dynasty was altered for the fourth championship in 1963, when lead Wes Richardson was replaced by Mel Perry. Being brothers (or sisters) is similar to being teammates, but when it comes to curling they must be teammates first.

The Role of Personality

Personality plays a significant role in teamwork, and the relationship between it and sport performance has been well studied. One current and widely accepted view is that we are born with a range of personality tendencies, called traits, which help make us unique. Inherited traits, like competitiveness or extroversion, are influenced by the environment over time. Senior curlers, for example, often describe how they don't have the same competitive fire that they had when they were younger.

Personality is characterized, in large part, by how we define and present ourselves publicly. Other people assign traits to us based on their observations of how we communicate and behave. The similarity between what we believe our personality to be and what other people perceive it to be depends on how well we know each other. Even then, the correlation is not perfect. In curling, one of the most comforting aspects of competition (especially during times of high tension) is having teammates who behave predictably. A third who is consistently reassuring is appreciated by her teammates when the skip has to make a particularly difficult final shot. On the other hand, what makes all relationships stimulating (and sometimes frustrating) is that people we know well sometimes behave in unexpected ways. For example, an outburst by a teammate who is normally calm and controlled elicits surprise because it is out of character.

If two people with dissimilar traits face a similar situation, they will behave differently. For example, if a rock "picks" at a crucial time, one curler may show emotion while his teammate remains calm. If two people with similar traits face different situations, they will also behave differently. For example, two equally competitive curlers, one on the ice at a crucial moment in a game and the other chatting with friends after an earlier win, will demonstrate far different behaviours because their immediate environment is different. In effect, our traits help us manage our environment, and, in turn, the environment interacts with our traits and causes us to behave in certain ways.

Several traits come into play when you compete: mental toughness, confidence, self-esteem, and persistence to name a few. A number of these affect curling performance, and five of the most important are described next. (To learn more about personality traits, see the Recommended Readings.) Other aspects of the first three traits are discussed earlier in the book.

- **The Will to Win:** Curlers who have a high will to win perform better in competition. They curl best in important games and are more likely to lapse when an outcome is not crucial. This is why some very competitive curlers don't enjoy or curl as well in club

or social games but rise to the occasion
when the stakes are high.

- **The Need to Achieve:** Those with a
  high need for achievement perform best
  when a challenge is difficult but
  potentially attainable. They lose interest
  and are less successful when goals are
  impossibly difficult or too easy.

- **The Ability to Manage Conflict Well:**
  Earlier in this chapter, you took a test to
  identify how you tend to manage
  conflict. Knowing your tendencies and
  those of your teammates helps you
  understand and, hopefully, tolerate
  strategies for resolving conflict that
  differ from yours. For instance, if your
  conflict-management style is
  "smoothing," your reaction to a
  frustrated teammate will be quite
  different than if it is "confronting." Your
  team needs both you and your
  teammate, so try to appreciate your
  differences.

Two other traits—introversion-extroversion and leadership—have yet to be mentioned. These are discussed in
more detail.

Introversion-Extroversion

A number of researchers have studied introversion-extroversion in sport.[16]

In general, extroverts seek stimulation in the form of serious competition and, compared to introverts, are higher risk-takers, more assertive, and more outgoing. Extroverts are inclined toward team sports, whereas introverts are attracted to more isolated activities, like distance running. Their preferences must be considered cautiously, however, because exceptions exist within different sport groups. For example, curlers, as a group, are more extroverted than most distance runners but not all curlers are extroverted to the same degree. Some teams, for example, remain at the rink to socialize after a game; others head home or back to the hotel. Differences also exist within teams. One curler wants to remain at the rink with friends while a teammate is ready to leave. That, in itself, is a minor inconvenience unless staying at the rink is interpreted as a lack of serious commitment to team goals.

The trait of introversion versus extroversion is important because it affects three major competitive needs: task, group maintenance, and individual.

- **Task**: On competitive foursomes, task need usually means the need to win. With recreational curlers, the need for on-ice success is balanced by an equal need to socialize. The section on goal-setting found

later in this chapter has guidelines on how
to keep your task needs consistent with
your team goals. If they are not consistent,
teamwork is compromised. For example, if a
new curler on a recreational team treats
each game like a Brier final, it may upset
more extroverted team members who are
out both to have fun and to try to win.

- **Group Maintenance**: Teamwork can't exist
  until the needs of the group are addressed.
  In other words, how does a team maintain
  its reputation, its scheduling, and the
  resources it needs to compete, to give just
  three examples? Difficulties in group
  maintenance can threaten teamwork. The
  earlier example in which the skip and the
  third switched positions temporarily
  compromised the team's maintenance need
  when the name change to the new skip
  confused the egos and affected the identity
  of two players. Fortunately, a balance was
  quickly reestablished and the team achieved
  its goal of earning a Canada Games berth.

- **Individual:** Although teamwork improves
  when members commit to meeting task and
  team-maintenance needs, teams are made
  up of individuals who also have needs.
  Curlers whose individual needs for
  recognition, respect, and approval are met

gain personal satisfaction that keeps them committed to their teammates and their team goals.

- **Recognition:** Curlers need to be recognized for the contribution each makes to their team. Along with the fame associated with being part of the Randy Ferbey foursome, Scott Pfeifer and Marcel Rocque are one of the best brushing pairs in curling. This gives them their own identity within a superb team.

- **Respect:** Good shot making ensures respect on a curling team. Curlers who show consistency game in and game out and in making clutch shots will earn the respect of their teammates (and opponents). The flip side, of course, is that inconsistency over time erodes confidence and respect. Curlers will describe how they still "like" so-and-so as a person but no longer respect the individual's curling ability. All curlers go through periods of inconsistency, but the best players work out their on-ice problems to stay at a high level. Those who remain inconsistent despite serious practice are like a weak link in a chain. They fail to get the same respect accorded to their teammates, and the team goes into competition with a handicap.

Even so, changes to personnel should be made at the end of the season. To drop a player midway shows minimal respect for a curler who may have worked hard to be part of the team and must have had some potential to have been chosen in the first place.

- **Approval:** Compared to respect and recognition needs, which are met by performing well, the need for approval from teammates (and others) is more of a personal validation that sustains a player through the tough spots of any season. It's the glue that holds the team together. Although connectedness within most groups ranges from casual (fans at a game or theatre goers) to more formally structured (office groups, planning committees for a Scottie or Brier), sport teams are different. The disappointments and thrills of competition create an emotional connection between teammates, much of it based on unconditional approval.

Leadership

Leadership contributes to teamwork in curling just as it does in other team sports. But although curling has the same qualities of leadership as sports like basketball or softball, such as assuming responsibility and inspiring others, curling has different leadership roles and styles.

Leadership roles can be formal, quasi-formal, or informal. Coaches in most competitive sports (as opposed to recreational leagues) are formally appointed, with defined responsibilities and length of term, and are evaluated by management or a sport governing body. In curling, especially at the team level, coaching is more quasi-formal, with responsibilities negotiated between the coach and the team. Although coaches are appointed at the provincial and national levels, responsibilities still tend to be more consultative than assigned.

Sometimes, however, leadership results from an informal role that an athlete assumes on a team, instead of from a formal role like skipping or quarterbacking. The curler who helps resolve a misunderstanding between teammates provides leadership that helps keep the team cohesive. The leadership shown by the third who works well with the skip to ensure all strategy options are considered takes pressure off the skip and makes the team stronger. All curlers benefit from teammates who, by word and action, contribute a calming effect during trying times and lighten a difficult moment with a wisely chosen bit of humour. On most successful teams the skip is the recognized formal leader, but others find ways to contribute their own brands of informal leadership.

Generally speaking, there are three leadership styles: authoritarian, democratic, and laissez-faire. The authoritarian leader takes charge, issues directions, and assumes responsibility for outcomes. Input from others is neither sought nor offered. The leader with a democratic style provides structure and a climate that encourages suggestions from members. Everyone is involved in planning and executing the task. In the laissez-faire model, no one assumes responsibility and participants work as individuals.

One pioneering study[17] assessed the effects of these three leadership styles at a camp for boys. Three groups of ten-year-old boys were told to use material provided to make papier maché theatre masks. The group led by an authoritarian worked quickly and efficiently at first, but when the leader was called away, productivity dropped significantly because the boys in this group had been given no role in planning the task. Work under the democratic leader began slowly because everyone in the group discussed how they would work together to make the masks. When the leader was called away, productivity and morale remained high to the end of the task. As expected, the laissez-faire group performed the poorest. With no leadership, the effort was disorganized and chaotic.

Based on these and other findings and after observing the leadership styles of successful teams, I have concluded that the democratic leadership style is a good fit for a curling team, especially since the introduction of the four-rock rule internationally in 1992. This rule has made curling less straightforward—strategy is more complex, brushing is now vital to success, and decisions are more crucial.

Exceptionally successful skips like Glenn Howard, Sweden's Elizabet Gustafson, and world champion Kelly Scott have always brought their teammates into the decision-making process at crucial times. Their democratic approach works because responsibility is distributed, and curlers—whether they recognize it or not—are more committed to a shot they have helped to plan.

If your leadership preference is democratic, you will be most productive on a team where all teammates have input into important strategy decisions. An authoritarian style will work as long as your team is successful, and a laissez-faire style lends itself more to recreational curling.

To help you decide whether you prefer a democratic, authoritarian, or laissez-faire leadership style, complete the following questionnaire.

LEADERSHIP STYLE EXERCISE

For each of the following statements, check True (T) if you agree or False (F) if you disagree.

T	F	
__	__	1. I enjoy collaborating with others.
__	__	2. I am most comfortable when roles and responsibilities are clear and assigned.
__	__	3. I am flexible and able to change when circumstances dictate.
__	__	4. A team can be successful with minimal planning.
__	__	5. Curlers should be able to call their own shots.
__	__	6. I go along with the majority even if I prefer a different strategy.
__	__	7. When working with others, I enjoy telling them what to do.
__	__	8. I prefer to associate with people who take charge so I don't have as much responsibility.
__	__	9. I prefer to be on a team where we just go out to have fun.
__	__	10. I really enjoy club 'spiels where players switch teams and positions every few ends.
__	__	11. I prefer a "take charge" skip.
__	__	12. Everyone's input is important when a decision is crucial.

True responses indicate the following leadership-style preferences:

Democratic:	Statements 1, 3, 6, 12
Authoritarian:	Statements 2, 7, 8, 11
Laissez-faire:	Statements 4, 5, 9, 10

PRODUCTIVE GOAL SETTING

In a competitive, often high-stakes, environment serious athletes complement their technical preparation with goals that they can measure to evaluate their improvement. This section explains the different types of goals and why goal setting is productive. It also provides you with guidelines for setting goals, as well as some examples.

Sport psychologist Daniel Gould[18] defined a goal as "attaining a specific standard of proficiency on a task, usually within a time limit." The purpose of goal setting is to improve performance (which research has confirmed). Goals provide a framework for practice and competition that allows an athlete to track progress that, as Gould notes, maintains motivation.

There are three types of goals. A task-specific goal focuses on one performance skill, for example, your in-turn or any other skill that you can measure and want to improve upon. Subjective goals are more personal, such as deciding to communicate more effectively as a team and, like task goals, have to be measurable. Outcome goals, like winning a bonspiel or a provincial or Canadian championship, are inspirational. All serious competitors aspire to achieve inspirational goals, but they also know that this type of goal must not be brought into competition. An outcome goal is something you dream about accomplishing, but—unlike performance-specific task and subjective goals—it's not much help in the middle of a game.

Goal setting works for a number of reasons.[19] First, a goal makes you focus on the essential components of a task. So instead of going on the ice to "do your best," you choose a drill and measure it. Second, having a goal forces you to work harder. If your practice goal is to make eight of ten take outs, throwing ten take outs requires more effort and concentration than deciding simply to throw a few hits. Third, you'll work longer and find it less boring if you have a specific measurable task. Finally, goals motivate you to try different strategies. If your goal is to slide straighter, you will tinker with foot positions, shoulder and hip alignment, and how you hold your brush until you find the combination that works for you.

How to Set Goals

Here are some suggestions to help you set your goals:

- Focus on performance goals, not outcome goals. These are the goals that will help you reach your dream, like representing your province at the Scottie or the Brier.

- State your goals in positive language. For example, your goal should be to make more shots, not have fewer misses. A goal to "have fewer misses" reflects negative thinking that you want to avoid.

- Choose task and subjective goals that are explicit (like achieving a percentage on a specific shot or changing your behaviour) and measurable. For a task-specific goal, start with a base measure that will be your standard for comparison. For example, aim for six consecutive draws to the four foot. Once you achieve six, try for seven.

- Have a strategy for achieving a goal (like ten consecutive out-turns added to your practice routine) and set a date to achieve it (80 per cent by Christmas).

- Prioritize your task and subjective goals. Those you consider crucial (like the correct release on your in-turn just prior to playdowns) need your immediate attention. Work on less important items later.

- Decide if your goals are short, medium, or long term. A short-term goal is one that you choose and measure during your next practice or game (or even the next shot). For your next club game, set a short-term goal to make 75 per cent of your shots. Medium goals may take you part of a season to achieve and long-term goals a full season or longer. A good way to accomplish your medium- and long-term goals is to set a series of consecutive short-term goals. For example, I know a curler who has set a three-year goal to improve his skill to the point where he has a chance to join a competitive team.

- Set challenging but realistic goals for both practice and competition and keep a record to track your progress. You'll lose motivation if a goal is too easy and be tempted to give up if it's too difficult. For example, if you currently average 65 per cent on your out-turns, reaching a consistent 80 per cent by the middle or end of the season is a realistic goal. Just remember that you're unlikely to be averaging 80 per cent within a few games. Instead, set a series of practice sessions where you throw a specific number of out-turns and track your success. As long as your delivery is technically consistent and you practise regularly, you should improve over time and be able to achieve an 80 per cent average by later in the season.

Examples of how to set and evaluate a task-specific and a subjective goal are included next. These are followed by a blank goal-setting form and an evaluation log you can use to track your progress in achieving your goals.

TASK-SPECIFIC GOAL

Current draw percentages average 60 per cent on in-turns and 68 per cent on out-turns

Goal: 75 per cent on both turns

Achievement Date: 31 December

Strategy
   1. Add ten consecutive draws to each practice.
   2. Alternate turns with each practice (to avoid staleness).

Method(s) of Assessment
   1. Record percentage at each practice.
   2. Record game percentages.

Method of Evaluation
   1. Track percentages on evaluation log.

SUBJECTIVE GOAL

Tendency to think negatively during a game

Goal: Lessen negative thinking

Achievement Date: Consistent progress,
   beginning immediately

Strategy
1. Keep track of negative thoughts during a game by making a mental note to myself.
2. Ask teammates to help me keep track of negative comments that suggest negative thinking.
3. Decide on the actual number of negative thoughts I had after the game.

Method(s) of Assessment
1. Record the number of negative thoughts I recalled.

Method of Evaluation
1. Track the number of thoughts on the evaluation log with the goal of having the number decline.

GOAL SETTING

Goal:

Achievement Date:

Strategy

1.

2.

3.

4.

5.

Method(s) of Assessment

1.

2.

3.

4.

5.

Method(s) of Evaluation

1.

2.

3.

GOAL-EVALUATION LOG

Goal-setting Progress (P) 1–5 (1 = very poor; 3 = average; 5 = excellent)

Date	Game (G) Practice (P)	Goal 1:	P	Goal 2:	P	Goal 3:	P

Some Final Thoughts on Goal Setting

You can work on several goals at one time. Just make sure that each goal is specific and measurable and that you track your progress.

If your progress slows as you work toward a goal, you've likely reached a plateau where more practice won't help in the short term. If this happens, work on a new goal and return to the other goal in a week or so.

Always be prepared to revise your goals. If you achieve a goal more quickly than you planned, make your goal more difficult. For example, if you reach your goal of averaging 75 per cent on your draws two weeks ahead of schedule, take a brief break from draw drills. After a few days, set a new goal of 80 per cent and return to your drills. If your progress is slower than anticipated, make your goal a little easier. Set goals are estimates, not absolutes. Once you've achieved the lowered standard, set your goal to the next level.

Subjective goals are harder to measure, so you need to find creative ways to gauge your progress. If, for example, you want to eliminate negative talk or thoughts during games, buy a counter that golfers use to track the number of shots they take. Keep it in your pocket and record each negative thought or comment you make. One team used a financial incentive. Any team member who made a negative comment had to put twenty-five cents in the team bank. The quarters were counted regularly—the long-term goal, of course, was fewer quarters in the bank—and the money was used for team treats.

The three tools described in this chapter—effective communication, cohesive teamwork, and productive goal setting—will help you develop mental toughness, improve your team dynamics, and, combined with your shot-making skills, increase your chances of competitive success. But despite your hard work, there will likely be some bumps in your road to success. In the next chapter, you'll learn how you and your teammates can minimize any challenges you may encounter.

Challenges to Success

Curlers compete for many reasons—the satisfaction of a well-played shot, the emotional connection with teammates after an exciting game, the challenge of pursuing difficult goals, and, ultimately, the enjoyment of the rewards that accompany success. The passion for the game comes from these inducements, all of them tangible and personal. They contribute to the longevity of curlers like Russ Howard and Colleen Jones and motivate the shot-making of Olympians like Sweden's Annette Norberg and Brad Gushue.

Although competitive curlers thrive on the challenges that the game offers, they know from experience that goals are not always met and each potential positive experience has a flip side. Making a difficult shot builds confidence; missing creates doubt. Winning unites teammates; losing challenges relationships. Achieving goals is rewarding; falling short is frustrating. Earning a provincial championship ensures a lasting legacy; finishing second promises painful memories.

You and your teammates can minimize the negative consequences of competition that you are likely to encounter. It involves maintaining your confidence, appreciating the value of practice, defining your expectations and commitments in writing, and dealing effectively with common challenges, whether game related or personal.

MAINTAINING YOUR CONFIDENCE

Of all the psychological attributes that curlers bring to competition, self-confidence is the most important. Like our other personality traits, we inherit predispositions toward confidence that are influenced by our experience and the environment. Some babies, for example, show little fear when exploring new surroundings. Other babies are more cautious but often begin to show more confidence after some tentative exploring. The same is true of athletes. Some display great assurance that is not easily shaken. Less confident athletes become more self-assured with success but also lose confidence more easily when facing real or imagined failure. Whether we study babies or curlers, individual differences exist, and they are influenced by events.

Our confidence is shaped over time by experiences that affect how we think about ourselves. We also experience temporary fluctuations in our confidence level. Recall how it felt to miss a shot only to be asked soon after to attempt the same shot again. Tricky, inconsistent playing conditions can test the confidence of the most self-assured competitors. Self-confidence, although a relatively stable trait, fluctuates according to circumstances, but successful curlers learn to keep these fluctuations manageable.

Most sport research shows a direct correlation between self-confidence and success. As well as helping to maintain motivation and assist curlers technically, self-talk can also be applied to confidence. Sport psychologists Linda Bunker and Jean Williams[20] proposed using self-talk as a tool to improve and maintain confidence; Kay Porter[21] described an affirmation as "a positive self-statement that is usually not true at the time but supports what you want to be true."

As you know from Chapter 2, when you construct self-talk statements, you must always be realistic and make them positive, personally meaningful, and in the present tense. For example, if you know you are an average brusher, it's hard to convince yourself that you're the best. Instead, prepare statements that are achievable and genuine, such as:

+ "I'll speed up my brushing stroke for this game."

+ "I'll give the skip the split on every rock we throw except mine."

These are achievable goals that will help you see yourself as a better brusher without having to be the "best." Your confidence improves as you brush more effectively and time shots consistently.

Self-talk only works if you practise it regularly. If you tend to think negatively before a game to avoid being disappointed, you have to work hard to change that ingrained habit. If positive self-statements aren't working for you, try a different strategy. Ask yourself if continuing to dwell on something negative is in your best interest. Once you decide that negative affirmations are not helping, it can free you from those thoughts. You haven't changed your way of thinking yet, but you have decided what doesn't work. When you feel ready, try a positive statement or two to see how they fit. If you still resist, you may need to consult a sport psychologist to learn more about your thought pattern.

To help maintain your confidence, develop a list of confidence-building statements (changed and added to over time) to rehearse in practice and use before and during games. Any time you find yourself using a negative message, mentally "stop" it and replace it with one of these statements.

Recognizing and Overcoming Your Negative Thinking

You need to recognize negative thinking before you can overcome it with positive messages. There are two kinds of negative thinking: circumstantial and personal.

Circumstantial Thinking

Even though you're normally a confident curler, questioning and doubt can arise when you play poorly, especially over a prolonged time. Your negative thinking is tied to the immediate circumstances, however, and is not how you typically think. Using positive self-talk in your practices and games should help you out of your slump.

Several years ago I worked with a young goaltender who had lost his confidence. Although considered one of the best junior hockey prospects at the time, he ended up on a poor team where he faced forty to fifty shots every game. He could not stop them all and, as his goals-against average rose, he began to doubt his ability, and his confidence suffered. When I met him, he had been temporarily assigned to a much better team for a tournament but no longer trusted his skill. He kept referring to the "slump" he was in. I asked him to describe what he meant.

He defined his slump as sudden and unexpected, which was an important key to his problem. I asked him to consider that if the onset of his slump was sudden, then its end could be just as sudden. This was the ray of hope he needed. More important, the idea was simple and made sense, and we focused on the notion that his slump could end as suddenly as the next game. As we talked, he assumed a more positive posture and began to speak more assertively. That night, he was the first star of the game and played solidly for the rest of the tournament. The affirmation we chose for him was "My slump is ending now."

Personal Thinking

Some curlers have habitually negative ways of thinking, which they probably learned before ever stepping onto a sheet of ice. For example, some people constantly play down their efforts, but this self-deprecating modesty, if it persists, eats away at their confidence. Perfectionist tendencies can also erode self-worth. Although there's nothing wrong with wanting to make the perfect shot every time, not all shots will be perfect. Curlers who are hard on themselves after every attempt may be using this strategy as motivation. It can be motivating, but constant negativity sabotages confidence. As many serious competitors know, the most effective way to strive for perfection is to plan perfect shots, accept outcomes that aren't perfect, and get ready for the next shot.

Using perfectionism as a motivator and self-deprecation to avoid outshining teammates is fairly normal in athletes. A skip interviewed after making a marvelous shot to win a game responds, "The whole team played well." But other thoughts and feelings are not as rational. The most common —personalizing, entitlement, externalizing, absolutism, and generalizing—distort events and are of no help when a team wants to review recent experience to plan for the future.

> **Personalizing:** This is the tendency to view a remark or an event as being about you personally, even though it may not be. It focuses your attention away from your performance toward possibly inaccurate interpretations of remarks or events and can involve circumstances over which you may have little control. For example, if two of your teammates are huddled in

conversation, they are not necessarily criticizing the last rock you threw. Worse yet, you are now wondering what they are thinking instead of focusing on your next shot. This kind of thinking is self-defeating.

Entitlement: It's a mistake to think that outcomes should always be fair (rocks pick and opponents sometimes get lucky) and conditions ideal (ice can be tricky and rocks aren't always perfectly matched). It's far healthier to accept what you have no control over. You don't have to like what happened. Instead, think of it as a sign of personal strength to treat adversity as one more challenge and remember that it takes patience to cope with bad luck. Besides, breaks often even out during the course of a game.

A dramatic example of this occurred during the 2007 Brier. During the seventh draw, Newfoundland skip Brad Gushue's final shot on the tenth end was lost when his rock caught something. The game went to an extra end where fate intervened against Northern Ontario. Al Harnden and Brad Jacobs both lost rocks and Gushue won the game. Earlier, Saskatchewan skip Stephanie Lawton's "pick" of her last rock in the ninth end of the 2007 Provincial final against

Jan Betker cost her a three-ender and possibly the championship. The breaks did not even out that day, but mental toughness and not obsessing about "entitlement" will enable the Lawton team to overcome this disappointing setback. As World Champion and 1988 Olympic medalist Linda Moore cautioned, "Expect the unexpected."

Externalizing: Blaming ice, rocks, opponents, and teammates is not productive because it signals a reluctance to assume personal responsibility. Instead of assigning outside blame, use statements that are within your control:

> "Expecting life to treat you well because you are a good person is like expecting an angry bull not to charge because you are a vegetarian!"
>
> *Shari R. Barr*

"The ice is heavier in that spot. That's why we're missing."

vs

"I'll remember to throw more weight."

OR

"Why do I always get the mismatched rocks?"

vs

"I'll work with the skip to decide which rock to throw first."

and

"I am helping the team by doing this."

Absolutism: Curlers who see the world in black-and-white terms are absolutists. They categorize people and events according to two extremes: nice or not nice; bad or good. Once an opponent is labeled "unpleasant," he or she is forever defined that way. A game is either well or badly played, with no consideration given for variations in performance over ten ends. Categorizing and labeling—like personalizing—may be incorrect, and they serve only to distract curlers from performance-related evaluation. No one is unpleasant all the time, and some good things can usually be found in even a poorly played game.

Generalizing: Generalizing, one of the most common types of distortion, is easier to change than other thought patterns. Typically, it results from an athlete's overreaction to an event, which then affects how the athlete approaches similar circumstances. The golfer who has a bad game on a windy day tells himself (and others), "I never play well in the wind." Curlers tell themselves things like "We never have a good game against so–and–so" or "We don't curl well at the Granite."

If a generalization is based on only one or two experiences, a good team discussion can discredit it. One or two teammates who see the poor logic in the belief can influence a teammate to give it up. If a generalization is based on several experiences, introduce it into your practice until you overcome it. For example, if you don't play well at the Granite, practise there until you see that good shots are possible. Team discussions and on-ice experiences can disprove distortions.

Some Comments on Choking

A miss at the worst possible time, especially if it occurs more than once (like last rocks in successive games), raises the spectre of the "choke." Choking occurs for a reason, but explaining a miss as choking can label the so-called choker as mentally weak and unable to stand up to pressure. It's also an example of both absolutism and generalizing. The best curlers miss shots, sometimes important ones, yet not everyone is labeled a choker and not every miss is defined as a choke. The skip who misses his final shot in the tenth end to lose the game risks being defined that way, but an identical miss on the first end is unlikely to evoke the label. The title is assigned when performance failure occurs more than once at a crucial time.

Choking is a result of poor stress management combined with inappropriate concentration. In other words, when stress is not managed, a curler's focus can become distorted. For example, under stress, a curler who tends to focus too narrowly will miss important information, like the relationship between draw weight and when a rock begins to break, and a curler who tends to focus too broadly will have difficulty concentrating on the broom. Choking, then, is the result of an attentional problem directed internally (like being afraid of missing) where the external focus, either too narrow or too broad depending on the task, is induced by stress.

Some athletes are more prone to costly misses than others. Those who manage stress well and are more confident are at less risk. There is also a self-fulfilling prophecy at work: the more you worry about choking, the more likely you are to choke. This is because your focus is internal and personal rather than external (and broad or narrow, whichever is appropriate to the task).

You can decrease your chance of choking by:

- controlling your physical stress, using techniques like deep breathing and affirmations, like "relax"

- improving your cognitive awareness with statements like "I have made this shot before. I can do it again."

- focusing on execution, not the consequences of your shot

- simulating various shots in practice and pretending the stakes are high. (After winning the 2004 Brier in Saskatoon, Mark Dacey described how, as a teenager, he used to spend hours pretending that his practice shots at the Granite were to win the Brier.)

Building Your Confidence

Use the following worksheets to list statements that will increase your confidence and replace your negative thoughts. A few examples are provided.

CONFIDENCE-BUILDING STATEMENTS EXERCISE

1. This game will be tough, but I love a challenge.

2. I had good draw weight the last game. I will draw well again this game.

3.

4.

5.

6.

7.

8.

9.

10.

REPLACING NEGATIVE THOUGHTS
WITH POSITIVE THOUGHTS

NEGATIVE THOUGHTS   *POSITIVE THOUGHTS*

1. I'm afraid I'll   I've made this shot
   miss.   before.

2. Why do we   We'll get the next
   always get the   break.
   bad breaks?

3.

4.

5.

6.

7.

8.

9.

10.

THE VALUE OF PRACTICE

Consistent play brings curling success. Curlers who shoot 75 to 85 per cent game after game enjoy more success than those who shoot 60 to 90 per cent (making the occasional brilliant shot but just as likely missing routine opportunities). In general, most curlers prefer a steady teammate to one who is inconsistent.

There is no magic to becoming a consistent curler. Newer curlers practise to develop correct technique, become consistent, and develop a "feel" for the game. Experienced curlers work regularly to refine and maintain correct technique and fix any problems that arise. All successful curlers practise regularly and have a plan for each session. Just throwing rocks does not accomplish as much as heading onto the ice to work on specific skills. Develop a tentative practice schedule for the season, outlining what you want to work on each practice. As the season progresses, change the content and times of your practice if necessary. If a freeze drill is a scheduled part of your practice but you're having trouble with your release, change what you do in your regular session or find a new time to work on your release.

Practices don't have to be lengthy, but they should be frequent. Some teams set aside an hour or so every few weeks for a thorough workout with all members and the coach present. Longer practices give your team a chance to use video and other devices to look at team members' techniques in more depth. Sessions where you practise alone or with a coach or teammate can be thirty minutes or less. After the summer break, early season workouts may need to be longer. Once you've fine tuned your technical skills and the bonspiel schedule begins, shorter practices may work best. Curlers can usually fit short, frequent practices into their daily schedules.

Depending on where you live, finding practice ice and time can be a challenge. When I worked with the Sherry Anderson team in 2004, it was easy to find ice at the various clubs in Saskatoon. The next year, with the Allison Earl team in Calgary, I was struck by the extra effort the team had to invest to practise in a much larger city. Travel time, traffic, and ice availability made practising a much greater challenge for the Earl team. At the same time, if you're a serious curler, finding time to work on your game is crucial to your success. The winner of the 2005 Scott Tournament of Hearts, Manitoba skip Jennifer Jones, left her law office at noon nearly every day to practise at a nearby rink. Instead of corporate lunches with clients, Jennifer's diet consisted of in-turns and out-turns.

> "I am a great believer in luck—and the harder
> I work, the more I have of it."
> *Stephen Leacock*

Practice Tips

- Incorporate psychological tools into your practice sessions. Use imagery, various kinds of self-talk, and breathing exercises to relax. If you become comfortable with these tools in practice, they become a natural part of your game.

- Imitate competition. Mini-games—two against two—decrease the boredom that can result from drills. Have your coach set up shots to simulate an "opponent" who is playing perfectly and then play ends where each team member executes the appropriate shot. This is important experience for actual competition and an opportunity for strategy discussion.

- Play practice games against strong opponents from time to time. As well as giving you a chance to test yourself against good teams, these games provide a break from the routine of continuous practice.

USING CONTRACTS TO DEFINE TEAM EXPECTATIONS AND RESPONSIBILITIES

Teammates have expectations of each other and responsibilities to fulfill. Sometimes, I find it helpful to have each athlete on a team complete a contract. A number of years ago, I used contracting to produce better teamwork on a basketball team where issues between teammates had resulted in cliques. I've also used this technique with junior curling teams. For curling teams, I have each member provide a written list of what he or she expects from and is prepared to offer each teammate, both technically and personally (a sample worksheet is provided at the end of this section. You will need a separate worksheet for each teammate.).

Defining expectations and commitments is essential to a team's success. Putting interpersonal responsibilities in writing provides a framework for how the team will work together, and everyone becomes more accountable for following through on their promises. Contracts that are shared openly provide a good focus for team discussion because everyone knows what to expect from each other. Unreasonable expectations can be negotiated, which lessens the possibility for future misunderstandings. Finally, agreements can be reviewed from time to time and adjusted, if necessary, during the season.

Tips for Effective Contracting

- To keep responsibilities manageable, list only two or three priority items that you are prepared to commit to and that you expect your teammates to commit to. If another item seems crucial, add it to the bottom of the contract.

- As a team, **discuss** and **define** how you'll actually fulfill all of your identified expectations and commitments. If you're a third who is promising to support your skip, how will you do that? By staying positive? How will you discuss shot options? How will you offer your honest opinion? If you're a lead, how will you help with timing? Hog line to hog line? Hog line to tee line? On all shots but yours? Everything that you and your teammates offer each other and expect from each other must be stated clearly, using examples.

- Review your agreements occasionally. Some teams develop contracts that they never look at again. The initial awareness that the exercise generates weakens if promises are not revisited. When you develop your seasonal plan for practices and meetings, put "contract review" on the agenda at least monthly. This reminds everyone of their responsibilities and gives team members an opportunity to change their commitments, if necessary. If a teammate is not following through on a promise, instead of avoiding the issue, bring it up as a normal agenda item. Involve your coach as a neutral party if it's a serious problem. On the positive side, morale is boosted when teammates are reminded that they are following through on their promises.

TEAM CONTRACT

What Do I Need and What Will I Contribute

*Name: Skip*_____

Teammate: Third_____

NEED FROM	WILL CONTRIBUTE
TECHNICALLY	
Look at all strategy options	*Discussion on complex shots*
1.	1.
2.	2.
3.	3.

PERSONALLY	
Support final decision	*Positive talk*
1.	1.
2.	2.
3.	3.

Teammate: Second_____

NEED FROM	WILL CONTRIBUTE
TECHNICALLY	
Accurate timing on rocks	*Read the ice well*
1.	1.
2.	2.
3.	3.

PERSONALLY

*Occasional humour to
lighten moments*

1.

2.

3.

Listen to suggestions

1.

2.

3.

Teammate: Lead_____

NEED FROM

WILL CONTRIBUTE

TECHNICALLY

Good guards

1.

2.

3.

Accurate icing

1.

2.

3.

PERSONALLY

Work well with second

1.

2.

3.

Input into strategy

1.

2.

3.

OTHER NEEDS AND CONTRIBUTIONS

1.

2.

3.

4.

DEALING WITH NEGATIVE CHALLENGES

People curl because they love the challenges that the game offers. Each successful shot provides a moment of satisfaction, whether you've thrown the rock or helped brush it into position. Collaboration with teammates and the expectation of civility from opponents are a large part of the game's appeal. Except for rare instances, curlers follow and enforce the rules themselves.

The game also has some potentially negative challenges—some game related, others personal. Being aware of these challenges will help you learn how to manage them more effectively and improve your game.

Game-related Challenges

Starting Well

It's important to start a game well. Of course, things don't always work out, but any early advantage like holding an opponent with last rock to one point on the first end or counting at least two if you have last rock is a good start on the scoreboard and generates confidence.

Major competitions allow practice prior to each game. Getting a feel for weight, reading the ice, and timing shots will help you and your teammates get off to a good start. For competitions that don't provide practice time, you'll need a different strategy. Some teams arrive early enough to watch the final ends of a game on the sheet they'll be playing on so they can time rocks and see how the ice is running. Whether or not you have pre-game practice time, always do a pre-game warm up. Your physical warm up is appropriate stretching and flexibility exercises. (Ask your local or provincial association to refer you to a fitness specialist who understands the physical demands of curling.) Your mental warm up includes self-talk and imagery to review your delivery cues, the stress-management techniques that work for you, and your motivational affirmations.

A brief team huddle before going on the ice gives you and your teammates time to reinforce your plans for the game and confirm each individual's game focus. For the first end, your goals and scoring objectives should be basic. Everyone should focus on making one shot at a time—but always expect to make both shots. Even if this doesn't work out, you should all be focusing on execution, not early game jitters. Some curlers make their first-end goal (which can be applied to every end) to outplay their opponent playing the same position. Team goals for the first end should include timing shots, reading the ice, and communicating effectively. Getting into an early routine in these key areas helps you prevent lapses in later ends.

Protecting a Lead

The four-rock rule makes it more difficult to protect a lead, especially early in the game. An overall plan to score at least two points with last rock or hold your opponent to one helps protect a lead because it maintains a game focus where risk is modest and strategy decisions are manageable. A team with a big lead risks being lured into more aggressive play by an opponent desperate to get back into the game, with potentially disastrous results. Being overly conservative is equally risky if it shifts your game away from taking advantage of scoring opportunities that could maintain or increase your lead. Kelly Scott gave an informal clinic on protecting a lead during her final two games (the first against Jennifer Jones, the second against Jan Betker) at the 2007 Scottie. With an early four-point lead in both games, Kelly's skipping decisions were neither overly aggressive nor too cautious. She was not enticed into getting too many rocks in play, and she made sure to take advantage of any scoring opportunities that arose. This plan enabled her to protect her lead in both games en route to her second consecutive championship.

Gradually building a lead over several ends doesn't seem to be as distracting as suddenly scoring a big end. Without realizing it, some teams tend to "let up" once they are several points ahead. For many curlers, a sudden feeling of relief accompanies a big score, followed by a lessening of stress and a change in their intensity of concentration. If this happens to you or your team, remain focused on taking advantage of scoring opportunities and preventing multiple points being scored against you. In other words, keep concentrating on the game and not the scoreboard.

In the final game of the 2007 World championship, Team Canada, skipped by Glenn Howard, took a 4–0 lead in the first end against Germany's Andy Kapp. The Canadian team then played patiently and steadily, holding Kapp to single points on the third and fifth ends while waiting to take advantage of any scoring opportunities that arose. It happened on the sixth end. A score of three gave Canada an 8–2 lead and put the game out of reach. By remaining focused end by end, Glenn Howard, Richard Hart, Brent Laing, and Craig Savill used an early lead to good advantage en route to a World Championship.

If your opponent hasn't conceded the game, concentrate on appropriate calls, shot making, and effective brushing to protect your lead. Otherwise, even small errors give an opponent a chance to recover. Seeing a lead slip away generates extra anxiety that you don't need.

Catching Up

If the four-rock rule makes it harder to protect a lead, it also makes it easier to come back from a deficit. A different approach is needed to recover from a disastrous end. Simply put, you need to be more aggressive. First, try to lure your opponent into playing aggressively and, second, go for multiple points. The basic rule is: the more rocks in play, the better.

Having a large end scored against you early in the game leaves you time to catch up, but you must be patient. Teams often try to get points back immediately by taking greater risks than they need to. Instead, if several ends remain to be played, your goal should be to score two points (more is a bonus) with last rock. Then, try to force your opponent to take one point and go for multiple points again when you have last rock. If you're patient, within a few ends, you should be back in the game. Reserve your large-risk strategy for late in the game when you have no other options.

Ending Well

Your strategy for the final end depends on the score and who has last rock. But you can learn to manage your final shots—and end the game well—using teamwork and the appropriate psychological techniques. (If you want to improve your tactical game, attend curling clinics offered by your association or club.)

In close games or extra ends, even though the outcome of the game often depends on the final shots, what happens earlier in the end has a huge impact on the skip's success. The lead who splits a front rock to the side to open the four foot plays a significant role in what happens in the remainder of the end. The second who executes a double peel leaves easier shots and more strategy options for the third and the skip. Everyone's shots are always important, but even more so on the final end.

Because the object of a game is to win, it's impossible not to think about the score, especially in late ends. Some coaches tell their curlers to concentrate on making shots and not worry about the scoreboard, but this is unrealistic. Instead, check the score when it doesn't distract you from more important things. Teams often have a brief huddle after an end, and this is a good time to consider the score as part of your strategy for the next end. Everyone can then begin the next end concentrating on shot calls and execution, timing and brushing.

Although throwing draws, hits, and freezes on the final end is not technically different from the same attempts on the second or fifth ends, the consequences of missing are greater in the final end and add pressure that makes final shots more difficult. If you remind yourself that the technical demands are the same on any end and focus on execution and not the scoreboard, you have a much better chance of making your shots at any crucial point in the game. The final end, more than any other, requires a clear focus on technical delivery cues, good imagery, effective self-talk, and a deep breath or two to relax.

Knowing the Ice

Knowing the ice is an essential part of successful curling. Every team member, but especially the third and the skip, must learn the ice and be able to adapt quickly to changing conditions. In the final game of the 2004 Scott Tournament of Hearts in Red Deer, Alberta, Colleen Jones learned the ice conditions more quickly than Quebec's Marie-France Larouche. This gave Jones the advantage she needed to establish early control and claim her fourth consecutive championship.

With the four-rock rule, curlers can use the reliable, keen ice—with its considerable movement—to showcase a wide range of shots, such as the angle raises and pressure-filled draws to the button that we all marvel at. Inconsistent or very straight ice is a liability to skilled curlers because finesse and shot variety are compromised when consistent rock release doesn't matter and getting behind guards is impossible. The comment that "the ice is the same for both teams" may be true in theory, but not in real life. Straight or unreliable ice that reduces the number of shot options shortens the gap between good and average teams and is why favoured teams sometimes don't survive district or regional playdowns and long shots do.

Good teams appreciate and acknowledge good ice, but they also have a right to complain about poor ice conditions. At the same time, complaining about the ice won't change it. What you can change is your approach to the game—both your strategy and your attitude.

Strategically, you may need to change your game plan since trying to force shots that the ice won't give you is pointless. Instead of throwing your favourite precision shots, you may need to go to basic draws, hits, and straight raises on guards close to the house. You don't have to like the ice, but you can decide to manage and read it better than your opponents. Forcing them to play the falling turn or a draw that won't bury gives you advantages that may turn the game in your favour.

Maintaining a positive attitude under less-than-desirable playing conditions is difficult. It's frustrating when your well-thrown rocks don't end up where they should and the team you should dispose of easily is too close to you on the scoreboard. But instead of complaining or wishing things were different, take the attitude that the ice is one more challenge to be overcome and you'll take what it gives you. Be prepared to accept lower performance standards from yourself and your teammates and focus on doing whatever it takes to stay ahead of your opponent on the scoreboard.

> "We will either find a way or make one."
> *Hannibal*

Personal Challenges

Balancing Demands

Like most curlers, you probably have demands in your life that are unrelated to competition. The stress management section in Chapter 1 includes strategies to cope with the everyday demands of life, such as work requirements that cause you to miss a Super League game or a child home from school with the flu. These temporary inconveniences to your curling career are basically time-management problems that you can minimize with planning, prioritizing, and a good support network.

Some personal demands are much larger and harder to balance with your competitive curling career, however. A job that takes you away from home for extended periods or a chronic family illness is an ongoing demand that can become an obstacle to your curling unless you develop a plan to manage it. If you don't do this, you risk falling into unproductive cycles of frustration and guilt that have you believing you are not performing adequately on the job, at home, or at the rink. To manage large demands, you need solid planning and, when possible, support from others. For example, during my team's championship years, our third, Sheila Rowan, cared for her widowed mother who was confined to a wheelchair. Strong support from family and friends who took care of Mrs. Rowan and brought her to the rink for our important games made it easier for Sheila to concentrate on curling.

Good planning and the support of others are not enough to guarantee success, however. You still need to develop your own personal coping strategies. When demands seem numerous and obstacles large, a good strategy is to reflect on past experiences, on-ice and off, when you overcame difficulties. Reminding yourself how you've coped with adversity helps assure you that you can do it again and prepares you for any future adversity you may face, such as slumps, staleness, burnout, and choking.

Performance Killers

SLUMPS

Earlier in this chapter, we looked at the slump experienced by a goaltender: what caused it and how it was overcome. Like all athletes, curlers experience times when they don't play well. A slump usually starts with technical problems that alter a curler's mental approach to the game. Changes in shot execution, often small and subtle, result in half-shots and misses that, if they continue, negatively affect confidence. Slumps can also result from staleness. Many hours spent on the ice over a six month season can dilute anyone's enthusiasm for the game.

Remaining positive is easy when you're playing well. It's when you're not playing well that you begin to doubt yourself and lose confidence, a sequence that becomes a self-fulfilling prophecy. When you are in a slump, your goal should be to go into your next competition confident that you are sound technically and with a plan to rely on positive thoughts produced by positive self-talk.

Here are some strategies to help you overcome a slump:

- Start by asking your coach or a teammate who is good at assessment to evaluate the mechanics of your delivery (using video, if possible) to be sure that your mechanics are sound.

- Don't panic over two or three poor performances. Those happen to everyone. Worrying about poor play only makes the problem worse.

- If your slump lasts more than a few weeks, use the mental techniques you relied on when you were playing well: correct imagery, positive self-talk, and various stress-management strategies.

- Keep a long-term perspective on your game, recognizing that dips and plateaus happen to everyone. Recall times when you played well.

- Focus on things you can control, like working on your mechanics and your mental approach to competition. Don't worry about things you can't control, like ice conditions or a teammate's poor play.

- Get professional help if your slump drags on.

STALENESS

Staleness can cause a slump in performance, but its causes—which are primarily fatigue or boredom—are more mental than mechanical. Between early October and late March, serious curlers spend hundreds of hours on the ice both in regular practice and challenging competitions. If this routine continues without a break, competitors will almost certainly experience times when their enthusiasm declines and their performance suffers. (The importance of leaving the environment is discussed in Chapter 1.)

Here are three strategies that you and your teammates can use to combat staleness:

- Set a seasonal schedule that provides brief breaks to decrease the chance of staleness and increase the chance of peaking at appropriate times like important bonspiels and playdowns.

- Set measurable goals for practices and less important games. For example, try to make six successive draws around a guard to the four foot in front of the tee line (an important skill today). Being determined to be four ahead after five ends in a club game adds motivation to your efforts.

- Introduce variety into your practice routine. Throw rocks at different clubs to change your practice environment and experience different ice conditions. Arrange practice games against other teams where the focus is on certain shots (like draws, freezes, and tap backs but no hitting). This lets you practise these shots and be more creative with strategy. Team practices are more challenging if you add an end of two-against-two competition where the losers buy coffee. Olympian Russ Howard once described how he and his brother Glenn spent hours of practice time challenging each other during their championship years together.

BURNOUT

Burnout is a form of staleness, but severe burnout can cause a curler to drop out of competition. For curlers suffering from burnout, the prolonged stress of competition leads to physical and emotional exhaustion that destroys their motivation to compete. Athletes who tend to be perfectionists are the most susceptible. In curling, because excellence is attainable and perfection is rare, perfectionists face persistent frustration. They also tend to be overly concerned about what others think, which adds more unnecessary pressure, and compared with other high achievers are not good at simply accepting what happens on the ice and looking ahead to the next opportunity. They become exhausted because they have difficulty pacing themselves mentally. When this happens, curling becomes more drudgery than fun, and they leave the game.

Burnout can be overcome with downtime from competition. It's particularly important to recognize the early signs of staleness, which are usually indicated by a loss of motivation. If this happens to you, learn to take a break— between shots, between games, and between competitions. Even though mental fatigue can't be avoided (remember how drained you feel after a close game), taking regular breaks where you think about and involve yourself in activities that are not related to curling leads to a quicker recovery and prevents the staleness that can lead to burnout.

CHOKING

Although slumps, staleness, and burnout develop over time, a curler can be labeled a "choker" after only missing a few shots at a crucial time. To overcome "choking," you need to remember that it is caused by excessive motivation (stress) that leads to inappropriate concentration (whereas slumps and staleness are caused by too little motivation). Taking a break from competition won't help you stop missing key shots. What will help is using stress management techniques, combined with "anti-choke" affirmations, and concentrating on shot execution rather than outcome.

Problems with Teammates

Solid friendships enhance the curling experience, but teams can be successful without players being "best" friends. Certainly, the highs and lows of competition create a bond between teammates, but serious curlers will tell you that mutual trust and respect—performance related and personal—are what bind teammates into a cohesive unit. Curlers who trust each other accept a miss, expecting that the next attempt will be successful. They assume their teammates have the same competitive goals and believe what they tell them will not be shared with others. Teammates who respect each other can openly disagree about what shot to play but will fully support the final decision. Personal issues are raised directly rather than by complaining to others. Respectful curlers understand the difference between a disagreement and criticism and know that a disagreement is the more respectful strategy. Respect and trust take technical skill a long way.

These qualities are essential when it comes to deciding which position each curler will play, something that is ordinarily negotiated at the beginning of the season and evaluated before the next season. Curlers who fully understand the demands of each position and know their personal strengths and weaknesses are likely to accept a position where their skills will be most effective and will complement the different strengths of their teammates. A lead and second who are known to be good at judging weight will be of great help to a skip and third who can read ice well. The most successful teams are made up of players who are comfortable in their positions and have no desire to occupy the shoes of a teammate. The current slow but positive trend to maximize what each curler contributes to the team by moving away from traditional positional play has been mentioned before. Your team can be successful by being flexible and open minded to new strategies.

Sometimes, switching positions in mid-season may be a good option, for example, when a new team is formed or a new player is added to an existing team. This option should be discussed during a team meeting so that everyone can contribute and the added contribution that players can make by switching positions can be emphasized positively. Players on good teams recognize the importance of each position to team success and don't see a move as a demotion but as a strategy that is in the best interest of the team.

When and why should a team change personnel? Today, competitive curlers plan more carefully and make more long-range plans than in the past. Changes in team personnel are more dramatic now that curlers have lucrative opportunities like national and world championships, endorsements, and big money 'spiels, as well as the lure of Olympic gold. A curler leaving a team in mid-season is rare. Most curlers commit to a team for the season and use the year to evaluate whether the team should continue together. Curling's Olympic status has more teams planning for the longer term. Player moves seem to occur after an Olympics—skips Kevin Martin and Jeff Stoughton, for example, added new teammates after the 2006 Games with an eye toward the 2010 Olympics in Vancouver, British Columbia.

Curlers are dropped from or leave teams for a variety of reasons. Sometimes, a player's skill level is not equal to that of teammates. If the player does not improve despite dedicated effort, teammates become frustrated and the curler, unable to perform at a higher level, feels tremendous pressure. This is a case where it's better for the player to find a new team and the team another teammate.

Problems also arise when teammates don't have a similar commitment to the game. Those who are keen become discouraged and frustrated with a teammate who misses practice or plays down the importance of coaching, planning, and sport science to team development. Here, too, it's a good idea to recruit a new teammate who is more interested in investing the time needed to improve. Curling teams, whether seriously competitive or recreational, are more harmonious when everyone has a similar commitment to team goals.

When sensitive and serious personal issues develop between teammates, it may lead to a change in team personnel. If team members' skill levels and commitment to team goals are strong, every effort should be made to resolve the issues through mediation that involves the coach or a neutral facilitator. Splitting up a promising team should be a last resort. If, despite strong efforts to work things out, the personalities remain incompatible, it leaves no other option but separation. Treating each other respectfully is of paramount importance, especially since emotions may run strong in the circumstances. To rephrase a familiar maxim: Treat your teammates as you would like to be treated, whether you remain together for years or decide to seek new opportunities.

Will you adopt and consistently apply everything offered in this book? Since everything offered may not apply to your circumstances, perhaps not. A good alternative is to try out the strategies that fit you and your team's specific curling needs. They'll help you become a stronger and more successful competitor. Just remember to be patient if changes don't happen immediately. New thoughts, images, feelings, and behaviours have to be practised both off and on the ice to become effective enough to replace older, less productive mental strategies that have become habits. If this book helps you do that, then I've achieved my goal.

Recommended Readings

Albinson, J. G., and Bull, S. J. 1988. *A Mental Game Plan: A Training Program for All Sports.* London, ON: Spodym Publishers.

Atkinson, J. W., and Raynor, J. O. 1978. *Personality, Motivation and Achievement.* New York, NY: Hemisphere Publishing.

Butt, D. S. 1987. *Psychology of Sport: Second Edition.* New York, NY: Van Nostrand Reinhold.

Davis, M., Robbins Eshelman, E.,and McKay, M. 1995. *The Relaxation and Stress Reduction Workbook (fourth edition).* Oakland, CA: New Harbinger Publications.

Ellis, A. 1975. *A New Guide to Rational Living.* North Hollywood, CA: Wilshire Books.

Kauss, D. 2001. *Mastering Your Inner Game.* Windsor, ON: Human Kinetics.

Loehr, J. E. 1995. *The New Toughness Training for Sports.* Toronto, ON: Penguin Books Canada.

Porter, K. 2003. *The Mental Athlete.* Windsor, ON: Human Kinetics.

Ungerleider, S. 2005. *Mental Training for Peak Performance*. New York, NY: Rodale Publishers.

Williams, J. M. (ed.). 1986 *Applied Sport Psychology*. Palo Alto, CA: Mayfield Publishing.

Notes

1. J. E. Loehr, *The New Toughness Training for Sports* (Toronto, ON: Penguin Books Canada, 1995), 5.

2. Referred to as the Yerkes-Dodson law.

3. J. W. Atkinson and J. O. Raynor, *Personality, Motivation and Achievement* (New York, NY: Hemisphere Publishing, 1978).

4. For other strategies, see the Recommended Readings or consult with a sport psychologist.

5. For a more comprehensive inventory of these techniques, see M. Davis, E. Robbins Eshelman, and M. McKay, *The Relaxation and Stress Reduction Workbook*, 4th ed. (Oakland, CA: New Harbinger Publications, 1995).

6. Adapted from J. G. Albinson and S. J. Bull, *A Mental Game Plan: A Training Program for All Sports* (London, ON: Spodym Publishers, 1988).

7. See A. Ellis, *A New Guide to Rational Living* (North Hollywood, CA: Wilshire Books, 1975).

8. Based on the Homework Sheet developed by Davis, Robbins Eshelman, and McKay, *Relaxation and Stress Reduction Workbook*, 150–51.

9.In J. M. Williams, ed., *Applied Sport Psychology* (Palo Alto, CA: Mayfield Publishing, 1986), 272.

10. In Williams, *Applied Sport Psychology*, chapter 16.

11. S. Ungerleider, *Mental Training for Peak Performance* (New York, NY: Rodale Publishers, 2005).

12. Ungerleider, *Mental Training*, 25.

13. J. E. Loehr, *The New Toughness Training for Sports* (Toronto, ON: Penguin Books Canada, 1995), 5.

14. From David W. Johnson and Frank P. Johnson, *Joining Together: Group Therapy and Group Skills* (Upper Saddle River, NJ: Prentice-Hall, 1987).

15. Based on Johnson and Johnson, *Joining Together*, 271–74.

16. See D. S. Butt, *Psychology of Sport*, 2nd ed. (New York, NY: Van Nostrand Reinhold, 1978), chapter 9.

17. P. N. Middlebrook, *Social Psychology and Modern Life* (New York: Alfred A. Knopf, 1974), 512–13.

18. In Williams, *Applied Sport Psychology*, 134.

19. Gould referred to earlier work by Locke, in Williams, *Applied Sport Psychology*, 135.

20. In Williams, *Applied Sport Psychology*, chapter 15.

21. K. Porter, *The Mental Athlete* (Windsor, ON: Human Kinetics, 2003), 43.

Index

Note: The italicized *c* and *e* following page numbers refer to charts and exercises, respectively.

About the Author

Photo by Darrell Selb

Vera Pezer, Ph.D, is a four-time Canadian Ladies' Curling Champion, including three consecutive years as skip, as well as a Scott Tournament of Hearts and Olympic Curling coach. She received a Ph.D. in sports psychology from the University of Saskatchewan and lives in Saskatoon, where she assists athletes from numerous fields with mental training and strategy. Pezer has been inducted into the Saskatoon and Saskatchewan Sports Halls of Fame and the Canadian Curling Hall of Fame. At the 2004 Scott Tournament of Hearts in Red Deer she received the Joan Mead Award for her contribution to curling. In addition to her athletic honours in curling, Pezer is also a Canadian softball champion and a two-time member of the Saskatchewan Senior Women's golf team. In 2006 Pezer was presented with the Saskatchewan Centennial Medal. An associate vice-president emerita, in 2007 she was elected Chancellor of the University of Saskatchewan. Pezer is also the author of *The Stone Age: A Social History of Curling on the Prairies*.